W9-CBJ-223

"If you've tried umpteen ways to quit smoking and have always relapsed, this book gives you a no-gimmick way that can work . . . save yourself much frustration and depression and use this way *first*. It takes great savvy to outwit an addiction. Sandra Rutter has that savvy and is passing it on to you."

Abraham J. Twerski, M.D., Medical Director Emeritus
Gateway Rehabilitation Center, Aliquippa, PA

"Nobody ever quit smoking by wishing—they did it by working to change their behavior. Sandra Rutter knows behavior and knows what works in changing it. Get this book, read it, do what it says, and you will learn what all ex-smokers know about managing a smoke-free life."

Dr. David C. Devonis, Associate Professor of Psychology
Graceland University, Lamoni, Iowa

"It is not an easy task to extend the scientific insights on self-control from the behavioral laboratory to daily life. In tackling the issue of smoking cessation, Dr. Rutter provides such timely translation, creatively circumventing the obstacles that researchers rarely deal with but that those quitting smoking confront continuously."

Federico Sanabria, Ph.D.
Department of Psychology
University of Arizona

"Many people try to stop smoking but relapse despite their best efforts. Here, Dr. Rutter presents an effective way to quit that builds periodic relapse into its basic program. Every component of the program is based on well-established research in the science of behavior. Rather than using academic jargon, however, Rutter presents the program in commonsense terms with lots of concrete examples so it is readily accessible to any smoker who wants to quit."

John Nevin, Professor of Psychology (Emeritus)
University of New Hampshire

QUIT BEFORE YOU KNOW IT

QUIT | BEFORE YOU KNOW IT

THE STRESS-FREE, GUILT-FREE WAY TO STOP SMOKING—
By Planning Your Relapses

SANDRA RUTTER, PH.D.

Hazelden
Center City, Minnesota 55012-0176

1-800-328-0094
1-651-213-4590 (Fax)
www.hazelden.org

Library of Congress Cataloging-in-Publication Data

Rutter, Sandra, 1941–
    Quit before you know it: the stress-free, guilt-free way to
stop smoking—by planning your relapses / Sandra Rutter.
        p. cm.
    Includes index.
    ISBN-10: 1-59285-315-3
    ISBN-13: 978-1-59285-315-1 (paperback)
        1. Smoking cessation. 2. Smoking—Prevention.
        3. Behavior therapy. I. Title.

RC567.R89 2006
616.86'506—dc22

                                        2005052505

10 09 08 07 06   6 5 4 3 2 1

Cover design by David Spohn
Interior design by Ann Sudmeier
Typesetting by Stanton Publication Services, Inc.

for NATHAN, ZOE, *and* SIMON

Contents

Acknowledgments

I am indebted to William Baum and John Nevin, who gave me support and encouragement from the inception of my research. Their assistance has been invaluable. Many thanks—again.

My deep appreciation also goes to the many researchers and physicians who took time away from their own workloads to read drafts of the manuscript as it took final shape.

I thank my agent, Drew Nederpelt at Metropol Literary Agency, for giving this book the opportunity to reach people who want to quit smoking, and for his all-around expertise and professionalism. Tracy Lutz, manuscript editor at Hazelden Publishing, contributed to the final draft with patience and good cheer. I particularly thank senior acquisitions editor Karen Chernyaev, who worked with me throughout the editing process. Her guiding hand kept the book on the right track, and she always kept in mind the best interests of the reader.

While I worked on the manuscript, Paul Jackson and Elizabeth Ezra allowed me to interrupt their family life with phone calls, e-mails, and visits to their home. Their kindness and consideration have been unfailing. Elizabeth has supported my work every step of the way, and I also dedicate this book to her.

Introduction

Why is it so hard to quit smoking?
"I just can't quit," some people say.
"I'm hooked on nicotine," other people say.
"Every time I quit smoking, I gain weight," still others say.
"Sometimes I quit for a day or two; once I quit for two years. I don't know what to do. It's hopeless."

No, it isn't hopeless. But if you feel that way, I'm glad that you and I have met, because I have a plan to end your craving for cigarettes.

"Oh, another plan."

Yes, a plan. But don't worry. I'm not going to tell you how to quit smoking.

"Well, I guess I'm looking at the wrong book. I thought I was going to find out how to quit smoking."

You *know* how to quit smoking! Most likely, you're an expert when it comes to quitting smoking.

"If I'm such an expert, why am I still smoking?"

Two things always happen after you quit. First, some time after you smoke your "last" cigarette—an hour, a day, a week, a year, or even longer—you smoke. Maybe you only take a puff; maybe you go all out and buy a pack of cigarettes. Second, you can't quit again. You smoke another and another and, before you know it, you're smoking as much as ever.

"So far, you haven't told me anything I don't already know."

Let's talk about the first puff you take after you promised yourself that you would never smoke again. Why do you take that first puff? That's an easy one.

"Sometimes I can't get smoking off my mind, so I know it's only a matter of time before I light up again. Other times, I think I'm doing okay and then all of a sudden I want a cigarette more than anything in the world. It just hits me."

When you quit smoking, you're walking on eggshells. You know from experience that even if you haven't smoked in a long time, you can be taken off guard at any moment. Living with this constant fear of failure can cause tremendous stress, and *stress* is one of the roadblocks that keeps you from quitting for good. Add that to the stress you already face in your day-to-day life, and it's just too much. You have a cigarette to make yourself feel better. Smoking relieves the stress, gives you a little energy boost, and, let's face it, much of the time is enjoyable.

Giving up cigarettes doesn't mean you have to give up pleasure or comfort and put on weight. The plan outlined in this book won't sap your energy, cause you to overeat, or leave you feeling just plain miserable. You will lose your fear of failure because at first, the plan *requires* you to "fail"—to smoke. When you lose your fear of failing, you'll also lose most of the discomfort of quitting because you will no longer be afraid of relapse.

"I've failed at quitting smoking so many times; I don't want to fail again. I can't see the point in going through that again."

What do you think would happen if you wanted to quit smoking, but you weren't afraid to fail?

"I don't know. Maybe quitting would be easier, but I'd still smoke again. I suppose it would also be easier to quit again."

That's exactly what happens!

"One of my biggest problems when I quit smoking, though, is that I gain weight. I can feel my clothes getting tight and then I get afraid."

You won't gain weight with my plan to quit smoking, because you aren't going to have to turn to food to stay away from cigarettes.

"Will I need to get a prescription from my doctor in order to follow this plan?"

No, no. The drugs, the patch, the gum—those don't work for everyone, and you've probably tried them. My plan is easy to follow; you can fit it into your life with almost no discomfort. And you won't need drugs or gimmicks.

"So you're saying that I can quit smoking without gaining weight and without taking drugs. Your book must be about improving my willpower. Sorry; been there, done that."

You don't need willpower on this plan.

"No drugs, no willpower. Okay, then this is about hypnosis."

No, that doesn't usually work either.

"Well, I can't think of anything else except maybe some kind of 'magical' new formula they're always advertising in magazines. And I've thrown away a lot of money on those."

Not that either. My plan is a new way of quitting. It isn't about drugs, patches, gum, willpower, hypnosis, or "magic." My plan is about quitting smoking without gaining weight, without going into severe nicotine withdrawal, without craving cigarettes, and without having to be on guard for the rest of your life.

You are going to become a successful quitter *by smoking.* Not the way you're doing it now, of course. Right now, you are a successful smoker. To become a successful quitter, you need to become comfortable with the possibility that you may take that "first puff" again.

"I don't want to take that 'first' puff because every time I do, I end up smoking."

Yes, but how many times have you quit again a few days after you relapsed?

"Never. I've never been able to do that. Once I start smoking again, it takes a long time before I feel like trying to quit again."

The only way you can get over your fear of relapse is to actually relapse over and over again. On my plan you have to quit smoking and then fail many times.

"Sounds weird."

Not at all. You will do what you do best: quit smoking and then relapse. The difference is that your relapses will be planned.

"What's the point?"

That's a good question. The point is that you will learn how to quit soon after you fail—easily and painlessly. As a result, you will lose your fear of failure. When you lose your fear of failure, you are much less likely to overeat and much more likely to quit smoking for good.

Three things make people overeat when they quit smoking using "ordinary" methods:

1. They feel constantly stressed about the strong possibility of failing—again. Stress leads to overeating or smoking—or both.
2. The idea of quitting "forever" makes them feel miserable. People who give up something that keeps them busy and gives them comfort can become unhappy. When some people are unhappy, they eat to feel better.
3. Eating becomes a substitute for smoking. If you smoke a pack a day, you've been bringing a cigarette to your mouth almost two hundred times a day. When you stop the repetitive motion of smoking, you keep your hands and mouth busy by eating. It's no wonder that people eat more when they try to quit smoking.

"I never thought about that."

That's why it's so hard to quit smoking using conventional methods. And that's why so many people haven't been able to quit for good.

"But I want to give up smoking for good! How can I quit forever if I have to smoke?"

This plan will make you a quitter easily and without misery. And you are going to succeed as soon as you begin. At first, you will quit smoking only one day a week. Then you will relapse—smoke—the next day.

"So you want me to do what you say I'm an expert at doing: quit smoking; then you want me to do what I'm obviously an expert at doing: relapse, or start smoking again. When that happens I won't be afraid of failing, I won't be depressed, I won't have the 'empty-hand problem,' and I won't overeat."

Exactly.

"That doesn't make much sense. It still sounds like smoking."

Only some of the time. You will do what you've done in the past, but you will do it differently and without stress, depression, or overeating.

Let's talk about time for a moment. If you had your last cigarette thirty years ago, would you call yourself an ex-smoker?

"Of course."

What if after thirty years without a cigarette you smoke a cigarette? Are you still an ex-smoker?

"Well, that depends."

It depends on what?

"It depends on whether one cigarette leads to another and then to a pack, and then a carton, and then . . . well, you know."

Yes, I know. I think you mean that the person can't quit fairly soon.

"Yes. That's what I mean. Because if someone can't stop smoking, then that person has no control over it."

Exactly!

"But if someone can gain control over smoking, that means that person can quit."

Right again!

"I want to quit. That must mean that I don't have control over my smoking . . . Dr. Rutter, I already know that."

I am going to tell you how to gain control over your smoking. With this control, you win and tobacco loses.

"I still don't understand how that can happen."

The plan is going to help you gain control over smoking by eliminating the obstacles that have prevented you from being a successful quitter. First of all, you will be able to quit without suffering severe nicotine withdrawal. Right now, you are addicted to the chemicals in tobacco. But that isn't a good enough reason to keep you from quitting, because many people quit long enough for the chemicals to leave their systems, and they no longer have any physical craving for nicotine, tar, ammonia, insecticide, or any of the hundreds of other ingredients in cigarettes.

Nicotine withdrawal begins as soon as you exhale, and it slowly intensifies until you take your next puff. That's why you keep puffing, and that's one of the reasons you keep lighting up: to keep your nicotine at a certain "comfort" level in your body.

When you finish the cigarette, your body goes further into nicotine withdrawal until you light another cigarette. You know that the first puff on a new cigarette is the best puff. But if you haven't had a cigarette in a few months, you aren't lighting up because of what's in the tobacco.

Nicotine withdrawal is at its worst about three days after you smoke your last cigarette and then it gradually subsides. You may have been able to tough out withdrawal for a while in the past, but on this plan it will not cause you much trouble, even in the beginning. For the first three months on the plan, you will never go for longer than twenty-four hours without smoking. Your body's craving for nicotine will slowly decline because you are going to smoke less and less.

Another, and extremely important, obstacle standing between you and quitting is that cigarettes have been as much a part of your life as the tips of your fingers, the soles of your shoes, your morning coffee, TV, and your Internet password. Life without cigarettes can be pretty uncomfortable for a while, and an unbearable craving can sneak up on you when you least expect it. All the times in your life when you have usually smoked a cigarette—they're not going away.

You don't have to be afraid of temptation anymore, because smoking is in the plan. At the same time, the plan will gradually transform the life with cigarettes you have now into a life without cigarettes. What will keep you going over the next few months is the cigarette you're going to smoke the day after you quit. What will keep you going down the road is the confidence that comes with success—not as a quitter, but as a quitter after you relapse. Future success as a quitter depends upon your ability to control relapse.

As you slowly gain control over quitting, the tide turns, and that exhausting battle you have had with cigarettes is over. Tobacco will never again control your life, your time, your money, your hands, or your health. All the bases, all complications, are covered in this plan.

Part 1 | The Plan

1 | Why Other Methods Failed You *and Why This Plan Will Work*

When most smokers decide to quit, they usually start with the cold turkey method—they simply throw away their cigarettes and try to sweat it out with nothing except determination. Many smokers take this approach not only for their first attempt to quit, but for their second, fourth, seventh, eighteenth, and twentieth through fiftieth attempts (with a sidetrack here and there for something "new"). Cold turkey has been the self-help treatment of choice because it's cheap, it's free of gimmicks or people or plans, and it provides a sense of control.

Between cold turkey attempts, smokers try a variety of other methods to quit. The most popular include drug treatment, hypnosis, support groups, behavior modification, bets, punishment for smoking, and rewards for quitting after a certain length of time. Then there's that old standby—food.

Unfortunately, because we have always been able to turn to cigarettes for either physical or emotional comfort, quitting smoking can be like abandoning an old friend, and it usually lasts about as long as a New Year's resolution.

Smoking is like entering a room with a door that swings tightly shut behind you. If you stay out of the room you're okay, but once you enter you can feel hopelessly trapped.

Quitting smoking can be like taking diet pills to lose weight: you lose the pounds while you're taking the pills, but they come right back on after you stop. Like dieters who gain back more than the weight they lost, many people smoke more after they relapse than they did before they quit.

Failure is almost as unpleasant as quitting, and sometimes it takes years before a smoker tries to quit again. Failing is like getting an F on your report card: every time you fail to quit smoking, you rack up another F. You know what happens to kids who get a lot of Fs. After a while they stop trying. Adults are the same way.

That's good news for the tobacco companies, because they don't want you to quit smoking. Tobacco is big business that profits a lot of people, directly or indirectly:

- tobacco growers, brokers, and wholesalers
- cigarette manufacturers
- tobacco lobbyists
- advertisers
- medical researchers
- universities
- stockbrokers who are commissioned for selling tobacco stock
- people who own tobacco stock
- doctors and other people in the medical profession
- hospitals, most which are owned by businesses to turn a profit
- insurance companies
- dentists
- pharmaceutical companies and distributors
- manufacturers and sellers of medical equipment
- lawyers
- people in the quit-smoking business

If you smoke a pack of cigarettes a day, that's 20 cigarettes. Multiply that by the number of days in a year and you're smoking 7,300 or 7,320 cigarettes a year (you can do the math when it comes to the money). If you take 8 puffs on each cigarette, you're taking in close to 60,000 puffs of nicotine, tar, and other tasty chemicals, such as weed killer and ammonia, every year of your life. (If you smoke "light" cigarettes, you'll take fewer than 8 puffs on each cigarette because the tobacco is packed loosely.)

In ten years, you'll take about 600,000 puffs on 73,000 cigarettes. Now, at $4 a pack—just to round it off—you'll buy 3,650 packs of cigarettes. Over those ten years, you'll spend $14,600 on cigarettes; $1,460 in one year. That's after-tax money going into someone else's pocket. And that's just money from you!

If no one smoked, doctors would still have plenty of things to worry about, dentists would still be filling teeth, advertisers and stockbrokers would sell us high chairs and soap and clothing— and ex-smokers would have more money to buy them. Tobacco farmers in the United States are already diversifying their crops (although a lot of tobacco is now exported to other countries). When you quit smoking, the world will go on. Plus, you'll have more energy, money, and better health to deal with other things.

You will be a quitter when you follow the plan I've outlined in this book. You can succeed because, unlike methods you have tried before, this plan doesn't force you to constantly think about quitting smoking. Most people can't deal with that kind of stress for long. Quitting smoking should not be about misery and failure—quitting smoking should be about success.

Not only will you succeed on this plan, but you will discover that it is different from all the ordinary methods to quit smoking in other ways:

- You get relief from quitting. At first, you will be smoking most of the time.
- Because you're smoking most of the time, you have the opportunity to plan better ways—your ways—to manage your quitting.
- If you relapse after you become a quitter for months, years, decades from now, you can get right back on the plan.
- You will never feel like a failure. You're going to be like the student who always failed, then takes a class and gets an A. Wedged among all of those failures is a ray of hope, a burst of optimism, and a sense of accomplishment and success.

Now imagine that the student earns some more As. That is what will happen to you not long after you go on the plan, because your success will slowly expand. Quitting after smoking won't be an uphill battle and, psychologically, relapse will be as easy as pie. Being easy on yourself when you fail is as important as making quitting easy, and ultimately, you're going to quit for good.

To help you along, the plan identifies potential roadblocks to success and provides ways to either deal with them or bypass them altogether. You can even learn to use these roadblocks to your advantage so that success affects other areas of your life as well.

Some of the roadblocks may never trouble you; others might cause an occasional problem, but two or three roadblocks may corner you at the same time. Everyone is different; every situation is different from all the others. There isn't any "one size fits all" advice that applies to everyone. This book is filled with flexible solutions, suggestions, and strategies to help you handle almost any obstacle you might encounter on your road to success as a quitter.

There will be times when you'll miss your cigarettes; they've been an important part of your life for years. Cigarettes are something to hang on to, yet you're trying to let go. When you're lonely, when you walk into a room that's filled with cigarette smoke, when you feel unsure of yourself, or when you're bored to tears, the plan will be there to help you.

If you became anxious or depressed when you tried to quit smoking in the past, you don't have to worry—this won't happen when you're on the plan. The success you'll achieve is going to make you feel good about yourself. This plan to quit smoking will give you more support with less trouble than you've found using any other way to quit.

2 | Getting Started

What does everyone know about quitting?

- Most smokers try to quit "forever." Whether going cold turkey or tapering off over a few weeks, their primary goal is to quit smoking for good.
- Almost every smoker quits for at least a short time: ten minutes, twenty-two minutes, forty-six minutes, ninety minutes, three hours. So it's safe to say that almost every smoker can quit for at least a few minutes.
- Quitting forever is extremely hard to do. Most smokers eventually fail to do it.
- Having a cigarette after quitting forever is giving up and giving in, and—failing.

By scheduling relapses, or failures, you can gradually eliminate the control that cigarettes have over your life. You will schedule quitting, and plan your relapses over and over, until you gradually phase out smoking. On this plan you won't have to try so hard to quit because a cigarette is always just around the corner.

At first, most of your days will be smoking days, but you're going to get used to becoming a nonsmoker by quitting smoking for one day a week. Almost everyone can do that. Those who have too much trouble quitting for one day can use an alternative plan, which is outlined in chapter 5.

While you're quitting only one day a week, you will have plenty of time to find new ways to change some of your daily patterns.

When these patterns change, you won't need to smoke anymore. And by the time you get through reading this book, you will have all kinds of ideas to help you along.

As the weeks pass you will add more Quit Days to your week. In all likelihood, you will be off cigarettes in two or three months.

And here is the payoff, the real payoff of this plan: if and when you slip and have a cigarette, or two, or three, you will know how to quit again.

Gone forever will be the emotional pain you carry with you every time you "fail" to quit smoking. If there is a "next time," quitting will be easy, because you will still know how to do it.

Before You Begin

Before you start the plan, keep count of the number of cigarettes you smoke each day for about a week. Keep track in a convenient notebook or something you can carry with you. Your memory will fool you—many people underestimate the number of cigarettes they smoke just as they underestimate the number of calories in the foods they eat.

Your smoking record can be simple (how many cigarettes you smoke each day) or it can be detailed with a lot of information about your smoking habits, including when you're most likely to smoke. If you want, you can record the time and date of each cigarette, where and when it was smoked, and maybe how you felt before lighting up and after finishing the smoke. Records show patterns. Perhaps you smoke more when you're tense or bored; maybe you smoke only when you're with other people. Usually, the pattern can provide clues to help you make changes that will control your smoking.

Even if you don't want to write down a lot of details about your smoking, keep count of the number of cigarettes you smoke—just for a week. If you open a fresh pack every morning and smoke it up by the end of the day, it's fairly accurate to say that you smoke twenty cigarettes a day. If your smoking is less consistent, you might want to mark on the calendar, including the time of day, every time you open a new pack. As long as you don't borrow or give away cigarettes, your count will be accurate. If you share cigarettes with someone else, keep your cigarettes separate during the week you're counting.

Many busy, successful people keep careful track of what they do. Ernest Hemingway counted the words and pages he wrote, and he recorded his daily output on a chart he tacked up to a zebra hide. Before he took time off to go hunting, he increased his output for a few days so he could stick to his publishing deadlines.

Records tell us how we're doing. Bosses, teachers, and parents keep records of behavior, and if the boss can use records of your work to calculate your value to the company, you can use records to improve your life. Once you start the plan, you won't have to monitor your smoking—with one exception, which I'll mention later on.

3 | The Plan—Quitting for Life

Forever is a long, long time, and most quitters resume smoking sooner or later. If a plan is going to work, it has to be convenient and fit into your life the way it is *now*. With this plan, you're going to quit smoking and deliberately smoke again so many times that quitting will become a painless and convenient habit. Quitting will become NO BIG DEAL! You won't be afraid to quit, and you won't be afraid to fail.

Here's how you do it.

Step One: Quit Smoking One Day a Week
Look at the calendar and see what's ahead for you. There may be a holiday or family get-together coming up where you'll be around relatives who smoke. Maybe that event will take place on Thursday. Perhaps Mondays are particularly hectic for you. By all means, smoke on Monday and Thursday—for now. Instead, select a different day of the week, say Tuesday, to be your "Quit Day."

Every day of the week, with the exception of Tuesday (this is an example; you don't have to choose Tuesday), you can smoke as usual. But from the moment you wake up on Tuesday until the moment you wake up on Wednesday, you don't smoke. If you get up at 9:00 a.m. on your Quit Day and get up at 4:00 the next morning, that's still okay. On Wednesday morning, you resume smoking as usual until the following Tuesday, when you once again quit for an entire day.

On this plan you have to see smoking from a different angle, a different perspective, because you don't know how things will be tomorrow or next week or two years down the road. All that you can take care of right now is today—you cannot quit smoking tomorrow because tomorrow hasn't come yet. So if you can go for one day without a cigarette, that's perfect on this plan.

Mark the Calendar
Circle your Quit Days on the calendar for a month so you know when one's coming up and you can see your progress. At the end of the month, decide if you need to change your Quit Day; if Tuesdays are just not working out, try Wednesdays for the next month. Also, think about which day of the week would work to add as a second Quit Day.

If you smoke at all on your Quit Day, mark | | | on your calendar (one line for each cigarette smoked). Three lines mean that you smoked three cigarettes on your Quit Day. If you didn't smoke at all, put a gold star or a nice red heart on the calendar. You probably know what the heart stands for.

You won't have to keep track of smoking on smoking days because you won't smoke more than usual. People who follow the plan usually smoke the morning following their Quit Day but don't smoke more than usual, because the first cigarette satisfies any nicotine craving.

HELPER
Remain at step one for at least four weeks or a month before you move on to step two. Go without a cigarette for at least one entire day before you add another Quit Day to your week. Find your quitting pace. Don't go too fast or too slowly, but try to stretch yourself just a bit.

One Quit Day a week is a huge accomplishment—it's a galaxy removed from smoking every day. But when you're ready, move on to step two, where you'll be quitting for two days a week.

Step Two: Quit Smoking Two Days a Week
After at least four weeks of abstinence one day a week, if you're comfortable with what you're doing (and not doing), pick a second Quit Day. Now you will be quitting two days a week.

***

CAUTION!
Be sure your second Quit Day of the week isn't back-to-back with your first Quit Day. If you chose Tuesdays for step one, choose Sunday, Thursday, Friday, or Saturday for your second Quit Day. Again, look at the calendar and make sure that parties and holidays don't fall on your second Quit Day. When you're first quitting, you want to give yourself as many breaks as possible. Later on, you will attend events where you may have to be around smokers, but by then you will be able to handle those situations without smoking.

***

Keeping Track
Keep track of the days you're not smoking, and if you have a couple of cigarettes on a Quit Day, write it down. You want to see your progress on your Quit Days. Always keep in mind that this plan can be modified to help you no matter how much you smoke and how many times you have tried to quit in the past.

***

KEEP THIS IN MIND, TOO
Nicotine withdrawal won't be much of a problem for most people. Withdrawal peaks about three days after the last cigarette and then gradually eases up. On your Quit Days you may experience some symptoms of withdrawal, but physically you'll handle it better than you've handled it the other times you quit smoking and you'll have an easier time because you won't suffer from psychological withdrawal as well—the anxiety and depression you have felt when you were determined to "never smoke again." Tomorrow, you know, will be a smoking day, but if you need to break your Quit Day into smaller components, see the two alternatives in chapter 5.

SOMETHING TO THINK ABOUT

If you continue to smoke on Quit Days, think about changing a Quit Day or breaking it down into smaller components. You may prefer an alternative plan (see chapter 5).

Step Three: Quit Smoking Three Days a Week

After you feel comfortable with step two (give yourself as much time as you need—this isn't a race), select a third Quit Day and try to stick to it. You should give yourself at least four weeks to complete step three; however, some quitters take longer, and at this point, some quitters stop smoking altogether. Your ultimate goal is to stop smoking completely, not to rush through each step in this plan. Quit at the pace that is most comfortable for you.

HELPER

You get a break when your Quit Days are not back-to-back. Here are some possible schedules of Quit Days for step three:

- Sunday/Tuesday/Thursday or Friday
- Monday/Wednesday/Friday or Saturday

There are other combinations as well; just try to have a smoking day follow a Quit Day.

Of course, if you're ready for a bit of a challenge, try having two Quit Days back-to-back at this point. If you discover that's too long to go without a cigarette, don't push yourself; for now just have a smoking day follow a Quit Day.

What if you've managed to be smoke-free for two Quit Days a week but smoke more than you think you should on your third Quit Day?

Don't panic! Just stay at step two a little longer. That's all; it's no big deal.

> **CAUTION!**
> Don't try to make up for slips by quitting on a day you hadn't scheduled.

Step Four: Add Another Quit Day to the Week

With step four, you have at least two Quit Days in a row.

Before you move on to step four, I'll tell you what has been happening. Over the past few weeks you've begun to gain *confidence* in your ability to quit smoking. You've smoked, you've quit, you've smoked, you've quit, and *you* have been successful. You're beginning to feel that you can handle quitting because you know that you can slip (at least on a Quit Day) and not fall. And being able to go for an entire day without a cigarette boosts your confidence.

The Difference between Failure and Success

"Maybe other people can succeed but I can't."
  "I'm such a big failure."
  "I never do anything right."

> **HELPER**
> Is this going too fast? Back up. Go back to step two or step three. If you have to, return to step one. If you smoke on your Quit Day, try to stop after one cigarette or part of one.
>
> But what if you keep smoking another, then another, then another, and on and on? Record the number of cigarettes you smoke on your Quit Day. This may help you see whether you need to make some changes. Are you continuing to smoke because the Quit Day you've chosen is usually stressful? Try to pinpoint what's interfering with your success. Seeing the numbers on the calendar can help you find solutions.
>
> You don't want to? That's okay. As long as you know you're doing your best, you can look forward to trying again next week.

SOMETHING TO THINK ABOUT

It's time to do the math. Let's say that you're forty-five years old. Let's also say that you will never quit smoking and that you smoke a pack of cigarettes every day for the next thirty years. In thirty years you will smoke almost 11,000 packs of cigarettes. You will smoke about 219,150 cigarettes (don't forget leap years). You will inhale around two million puffs of nicotine, tar, insecticide, ammonia, and thousands of other assorted chemicals, some of which you use for cleaning the toilet.

If you have only one Quit Day a week for the next thirty years, you will cut down from 219,150 cigarettes to 187,950 cigarettes. It isn't perfect, but don't you think your body would be happier if it had to handle 31,200 fewer cigarettes in its lifetime? Go for what you can do. If you have two Quit Days a week for the next thirty years, you'd be smoking 156,750 cigarettes instead of 219,150 cigarettes. That's 62,400 fewer cigarettes, and that's impressive. You can go all the way and cut down to zero cigarettes, but in the meantime, Quit Days will give your heart and lungs a rest. What's more, your heart and lungs will show you their gratitude. A lot of people don't thank us when we're nice to them, but our body really goes all out to show its appreciation: Every step is a little easier, every breath a little deeper.

Did you say that? Maybe I was just talking to myself again.

Self-doubt creeps into almost everything we try to do. It can be destructive, or we can use it as an opportunity to try out new ways of thinking—even if we don't really believe we can succeed. Until 1954 no one we knew of had ever broken the four-minute mile. Why? It couldn't be done—the human body couldn't run that fast. Then, in 1954, Roger Bannister broke the four-minute mile.

Was he special? Was there something about his body that let him do the impossible? In some ways, perhaps. It helped, for example, that he was a lean man with a slow heartbeat and a large lung capacity. But today, the four-minute mile is broken all over the world, and with boring regularity—almost as boring as a successful climb to the peak of Mount Everest. No one on record ever reached the top of Everest until 1953 when Tenzing Norgay and Edmund Hillary scaled it. Since then, over thirteen hundred men and women, including people with severe disabilities, have made it to the top. The other night I listened to an interviewer talk with a totally blind man who had recently reached the summit of the world's tallest mountain.

The biggest predictor of failure is thinking that you don't have the magical inborn qualities that will allow you to succeed. Guess what? There aren't any magical inborn qualities for success. Life is a series of tasks to master and challenges to overcome. Always remember the sign "Everybody makes misteaks."

You will fail sometimes, and you need to keep going when it happens. (Are you mumbling, *"I don't fail sometimes, I fail all the time"*? . . . STOP IT!) Fear of failure, or feeling that control is slipping away, can fill you with negative emotions—piles and piles of them—and that, of course, only makes things worse. You feel trapped and you think the only way to get rid of those unpleasant feelings is to fail. You know that you'll be angry with yourself and you'll feel depressed, but at least you won't have to be anxious and stressed out because you're afraid of failing. Not having to worry about failure is failure's only advantage.

Don't be afraid to fail. You will.

Life is either a series of failures sandwiched between a bunch of successes or a series of successes sandwiched between a bunch of failures. There isn't any other way.

Before Colonel Sanders could get financing to start his chicken business, he knocked on 1,600 doors! What would have happened if he had said after the eight hundredth no, "I think that if I get a thousand no's, I should forget about it and go back to plucking chickens"—or whatever he did before he became world famous and really rich? Remember that only successful people fail.

On this Quit Plan, it's okay to fail because failure is part of the plan. After a Quit Day, you're required to "fail," to smoke. Failure is built right into this plan's success because when you have permission to fail, the fear and the negative emotions that go with it evaporate.

What should you do on your Quit Day if you really need a cigarette? Well, you don't really need one, but smoking has been such an important part of your life, sometimes you can't see any alternative. Remember, you only have to get through a few hours, because tomorrow morning the plan requires you to light up. If you feel that you're smoking more than you'd like on your first two or three Quit Days, see the next chapter for alternatives. Try at least two Quit Days before you decide to try an alternative plan. You need to give yourself a chance to succeed! When you decide that it's either going to be a fistful of cigarettes or a pie on your Quit Day, read chapter 13, "Roadblock #8—Fast Food, Junk Food, and Overeating."

Making Quit Days Work for You
1. If you smoke on your Quit Day, mark it on the calendar.
2. Keep track of your progress and see where you may need to make changes. That may include changing a Quit Day.
3. Remain at each step until you are smoke-free for an entire day.
4. Circle Quit Days on the calendar so that you know when one is coming up.
5. Separate your Quit Days by at least one smoking day for the first three steps.
6. If you think that you're smoking too much on Quit Days, see one of the alternative plans.
7. Don't make up for slips by quitting on a day you haven't scheduled.

4 | Your Quit Day

A successful Quit Day has to do two things for you:

1. It has to fit into your life without inconvenience. Where you live, how you live, and whatever you do, you have to be able to "customize" your Quit Day so that you can go about your regular activities without turning everything upside down.
2. It has to be comfortable. If quitting makes you nervous, unhappy, and cranky, it won't last. That's why most smokers eventually try things that are long on promise but short on delivery.

Convenience and comfort—that's what this quit plan is all about. And that's why this plan will become as comfortable and convenient as smoking.

When you are a new quitter, you

- can choose your Quit Day—a day that fits most easily into your life without inconvenience or discomfort
- will go without cigarettes only one day a week. Quitting for only one day eliminates the discomfort of sudden nicotine withdrawal
- have almost an entire week after your Quit Day to think about how you can make your next Quit Day even better
- will have time to deal with some of the problems that drive quitters on conventional plans back to their cigarettes
- won't be driven back to your cigarettes by physical longing and psychological desperation, because *tomorrow is a smoking day!*

As you add Quit Days, a number of things happen:

- Your success adds up.
- You lose your fear of slipping.
- If you slip, you get right back on track without feeling guilty, hopeless, or depressed.
- The confidence you gain from quitting smoking will affect other areas of your life.
- You will know for certain that if you have one or a whole bunch of cigarettes after not smoking for five years, you can begin at step one and be a quitter again. And it won't hurt.

Quit Day Success
Make Your Quit Days as Pleasant as Possible
Your Quit Days should be as pleasant as you can make them— within the constraints of the rest of your life. Sometimes we neglect to enjoy ourselves because we're busy, we forget how good it feels, or we say that we don't have enough money. But there are many inexpensive ways to treat yourself, and there are many things you can do that don't take much time.

Be Prepared for Cravings
You should not be bothered by strong cravings because nicotine withdrawal symptoms usually don't peak until about seventy-two hours after the last cigarette. But some people can't go more than an hour without having strong cravings for a cigarette. If they are an almost constant bother on your Quit Day, you might be happier if you use an alternative plan (see chapter 5).

Most new quitters have slight to moderate cravings for cigarettes—not only because they have begun nicotine withdrawal, but also because they're dealing with situations in their lives where they used to smoke. As Quit Days add up—and it takes a few Quit Days before most quitters feel entirely comfortable without smoking—cravings become less bothersome. This happens because nicotine is gradually losing its hold on them and they are gaining more confidence in their ability to quit.

Still, it's important to be prepared for any cravings that do come up. Keep the chewing gum, bottled water, Nerf balls, and castanets handy. Keep a list of things you could do instead of smoking. Also, compile a list of phone numbers of several non-smoking friends you can call when you have an urge to smoke. Better yet, create a network of other quitters you can call. Keep the movie schedule nearby and be prepared to hit a department store, a gym, or any place where smoking isn't allowed. Find out which coffee shops are nonsmoking and what their business hours are, so you won't seek one out in desperation at ten o'clock at night only to find it closed.

Treat Yourself to a Good Time

Save pleasures for your Quit Days, and have a lot of activities lined up you don't do on other days. If you enjoy dining out, going to the movies, or shopping, wait until Quit Days. Your Quit Day is for *you*; you're doing something really great, and you deserve plenty of good things to make it pleasant.

Make Sure You Have Rewards When You Need Them

You need to have rewards throughout the day that you can get to. Make a list of little rewards you can have when you're at work,

---

HELPER

If you feel like smoking, even though you have been enjoying your Quit Day, move on to another activity. Try taking your calculator with you instead of cigarettes and count down to the time you can technically smoke, which, for most people, is midnight. Counting down gives you something to do, a calculator keeps your hands busy, and every time you check your calculations, you have less time to wait until you can smoke. Then move on to something else.

and rewards you can have at home or anywhere you happen to be. It's important to always have items nearby to reward yourself with for not smoking for a while. And don't run out of them! An extensive list of rewards is given in chapter 11, page 92. Just about anything that gives you pleasure will work. One quitter bought several Far Side cartoon books (by Gary Larson), cut the books up into individual pages, and read just two cartoons after not smoking for fifteen minutes. Someone else reads comic books on Quit Days.

You may come up with some ideas you think are crazy *("Oh no, I can't do that!")*, but some of them will work. For more ideas about how to enjoy your Quit Day, see chapter 9, "Roadblock #4—Boredom," page 77.

Keep a piece of paper and a pen handy and, as you go through a few days, every time you find that you are enjoying something, write it down. You'll be surprised because the list is longer than you think. You can refer to the list until you know it by heart, and you can add to it as you discover new rewards. Then make sure to keep your rewards in stock!

Keep Most of Your Rewards Small
One of the problems with rewards is that there's usually not much keeping you from having both the reward and a cigarette. One solution is to have lots of small rewards instead of ones you'll indulge in no matter what. An example of a small reward is chewing gum. If you like it but aren't a habitual gum chewer, buy several packages the night before your Quit Day. Gum keeps your mouth busy, which can be a big help. Then, don't chew gum on smoking days. On the other hand, if a pint of Chunky Monkey is a big reward for you, don't use it as a Quit Day reward. Save it to enjoy simply because you love it and not for any other reason, such as not smoking. So keep your rewards for not smoking on Quit Days small.

Your Rewards Are Important. Take Them!
Remember to take your rewards! It's easy to forgo these little goodies because they're small. You think that the job well done is

enough of a reward. When you're quitting smoking, it isn't, so keep the little rewards coming down the line throughout your Quit Day. It's an act of self-care.

When You're Frustrated, Stop

If you reach a point where you say to yourself, *"I've had enough of this. I'm having a cigarette,"* stop for ten seconds, close your eyes, and take a couple of deep breaths (I don't know why they call them "cleansing breaths," but it sounds good). Then do something that you enjoy and that is good for you—even if you can only take a minute or two. Play some music, sing, or dance. Take a few deep breaths if you're around other people, and think about how a role model would handle the situation. The opportunities are endless, but keep a short list of ideas on hand for when you're too frustrated to think.

Spend Time with Your Family on Your Quit Day

One quitter included his children in his Quit Days by planning activities with them at times when he used to smoke. After he came home from work or coaching, he didn't light up; instead, he took out his guitar (which had been gathering dust in the attic) and played songs for them. Then they all sang—loudly and off-key. If you don't have children around, you might play a relaxation tape. Or put on some music and dance. Or sing. You should definitely schedule dancing and singing into your Quit Day—by yourself or with others.

Too Busy to Think about Enjoyment?

You have always had time to take care of your smoking, and now you can slowly make the switch to enjoyable activities on Quit Days. They don't have to last long—there are things you can do for a minute or two that can take the place of a cigarette.

Take a break every once in a while throughout your Quit Day—you know what's best for you, whether it's every fifteen minutes or every couple of hours—and do something nice for yourself. Every time you do something pleasant, such as calling

> **CAUTION!**
> - Quitting smoking should not interfere with your sex life, and you should not deprive yourself or a partner because you're having a Quit Day. However, if you do things to enhance sex, try to save them for Quit Days. Every once in a while, one quitter meets her partner for a tryst in a hotel. They check in separately, one of them a few minutes before the other.
> - Don't punish yourself for smoking. Punishment only works when it's severe and guaranteed. Quitting smoking is *not* an exercise in masochism, and punishment for smoking doesn't work anyway.
>
> People usually fall back into their old ways because the old ways are more comfortable, especially if the new way involves punishment. Instead of punishment, it's much more helpful if you line up lots of little rewards just for Quit Days.

up a friend, dropping a Hershey's Kiss in your cup of coffee, or brushing your teeth with fancy (which means expensive) toothpaste, you'll associate pleasure with not smoking.

Be Prepared for Roadblocks

You will have them—coffee breaks, friends who smoke, your spouse who smokes—and you're going to have to deal with them one way or another. Fourteen roadblocks can affect you during a Quit Day (see chapters 6–19). Most people don't have a problem with all of them, but you never know when you will be caught off guard. Here's an example of something that one quitter was not prepared for:

Ben was doing very well; he stopped smoking altogether after he had been quitting successfully three days a week, and he hadn't had a cigarette in several months. He was absolutely positive that he would never smoke again (*big* mistake). Then he had an interview for a really good job, one he had always dreamed of but never thought he would get. Ben went in to the interview—Wow! The office was stunning, the pay was fantastic, the CEO looked even more impressive than his pictures in the newspapers. Ben was nervous; he sat down. The CEO took a cigarette out and held the pack out to him without saying a word.

Ben didn't miss a beat. "Thanks." Then he realized he didn't have a lighter with him. "!**#!," he thought. "I blew this one."

The CEO lit his cigarette. The two of them had a nice smoke.

No one can plan ahead for something like that.

Most problems have solutions. You can get through your interview or coffee break, you don't have to give up your friends, and you can remain a quitter after you return to the parking lot and see what someone did to the side of your car (which was parked very carefully between the lines). Part 2, "Roadblocks to Success," will offer ideas for getting past the challenges to your Quit Days without smoking.

Alternative Plans—
5 For Quitters Who Prefer a Shorter Quit Day

If, at first, quitting for an entire day is too long, that's not a problem. *Twenty-four hours are made up of 1,440 minutes,* and they can be spliced and diced in many different ways. No matter how you do it, what's important is that you strive for consistency. Try out an alternative plan for a few days and see how it works for you. If you don't feel you're getting anywhere, then go on to another one. What's important is that you regulate your smoking one way or another.

Perfect regulation for a quitter would mean never smoking at all, and that's your goal. But there are many roads to perfection, and all of them have been traveled successfully. Not every road to quitting is for everyone, and there are some that are great for a few; they are just less traveled. You may come up with one yourself.

Alternative #1

Smoke one cigarette every sixty minutes every day for several days. For now, you have no Quit Days; you smoke one cigarette an hour every day. There are different ways to do this, but be consistent.

Variation A

One way is to have the cigarette anytime within each hour. For example, on one day you might smoke your first cigarette at 7:05 a.m., your second cigarette at 8:15, your third at 9:02, your fourth at 10:25, and so on. I don't particularly recommend this method because it leaves you so much room to smoke whenever you feel like it. There is very little difference between smoking this way and smoking as you usually do. Still, this form of regulation is a start.

Variation B
A better way is to smoke one cigarette every hour you're awake at a specific time—whether you feel like smoking or not. The easiest way is to smoke the cigarette every hour exactly on the hour. If you wake up at 6:15, you wait until 7:00 to light up; then you have your next cigarette at 8:00, the next at 9:00, and so on throughout the day. The problem with this method is that if you always light up as soon as you wake up, then you probably won't wait until the top of the hour before you have your first cigarette. But here is a good solution:

Variation C
Get a watch with an alarm and begin your hour with your first cigarette of the day, whatever time that is. If you light up at 6:17 a.m., set your alarm to go off at 7:17, when you will have your second cigarette. Then you smoke your third cigarette at 8:17, and so on.

The advantage of this method is that it takes the thinking out of when you have your next cigarette. If smoking becomes automatic, then you won't have to spend your day asking yourself questions like, *"Now, what if I have five cigarettes right now, and then don't smoke for the next five hours?"* That makes a lot of sense when you'd like to smoke, and it's about as logical as the dieter who says, *"I could eat this half gallon of gourmet ice cream tonight and still lose weight as long as I fast for the next three days."*

The watch alarm takes over for you, just as your alarm clock wakes you up in the morning. It gives you more time to think about other things besides when you can smoke, and it begins to relieve some of the pressure you feel when you quit smoking.

Succeeding When You Smoke Once an Hour
After you smoke one cigarette an hour for several days or weeks—you have to judge how you feel about it—extend the quit time from every sixty minutes to, say, every sixty-five or seventy minutes. If you extend your quit time by five minutes, you might have your first cigarette at 7:00, your second at 8:05, your third at 9:10, and so on. Using the timing method, you can begin when you wake up, say at 7:12, smoke your second cigarette at 8:17, your third at 9:22, and so on. That way, you space your cigarettes sixty-five minutes apart.

When you become comfortable with sixty-five or seventy minutes, add another five minutes (or even less) of quit time. If you keep adding a few minutes to the space between cigarettes, eventually you will go an entire day without smoking. If you find that you're backsliding, slightly decrease the time between cigarettes for a while.

Even if you feel that you are still smoking too much, try to maintain equal intervals between cigarettes. If you can't go for fifteen minutes without a cigarette, try for ten minutes. When you do that, you smoke by the clock, whether or not you feel like lighting up. When the clock (or your watch alarm) has control over your smoking, you gain the upper hand.

Alternative #2
Quit for a certain period of time each day, say, between two and five in the afternoon. You can smoke as much as you want and whenever you want during the rest of the day, but for that set amount of time, you don't smoke. This gives you a fairly long period of time between cigarettes—almost like having a very short Quit Day—and it shows you that you can quit every day for a few hours. When you feel comfortable using this method, add a little time every week to your quit hours. Eventually, you won't smoke for most of the day; then, you'll be able to quit altogether.

"I Can't Do It"

If you still can't seem to change your smoking patterns, you probably smoke more than a pack a day. Maybe you're a chain-smoker. What would make you feel comfortable and, at the same time, help you to cut down?

Your first goal is to not cut down on your smoking but to begin smoking on a schedule. For example, let's say that Tony smokes two packs, or forty cigarettes, every day. Tony sometimes chain-smokes and sometimes takes time out to do other things.

If you smoke forty cigarettes a day and you sleep for eight hours, you are awake for 960 minutes. On average, you light up every 24 minutes. You can begin to quit by lighting a new cigarette every 24 minutes (using your watch alarm) no matter what you are doing. Eating dinner? Stop for a few minutes and smoke. At the movies? Go outside and have that cigarette. There are times, of course, when you can't jump up and leave what you are doing. If you are in a company meeting, you probably cannot leave; if you are a salaried employee with scheduled breaks, you can't always walk away from your post; and if you're sitting in the movies with two youngsters, you have to wait. This is where a little creativity will help you out. Your best strategy is to plan ahead and decide when you can smoke given the situation. If you have to sit through a two-hour meeting without a cigarette, decide in advance how much you will "make up for lost time"—and think about how good you will feel if you only have one cigarette instead of four in a row. In this case, time lost now is future time gained.

What on earth is the point? Smoking is one of the most important activities in your life. You probably do a lot of other things besides smoke, but your lighted cigarette goes along with you almost everywhere and you fit it in with almost everything you do. You don't believe you can quit smoking for twenty-four hours, and you probably don't think you can last an hour except when you absolutely have to. But you can cut down on your smoking by timing yourself because, instead of paying attention to the hundreds of environmental cues that lead you to a cigarette, your watch alarm tells you when to smoke. Once you give control of your smoking to the specific cue of an alarm, your body and behavior can adjust to the gradual decrease in smoking. Before you know it, you can add a minute or two to your space between cigarettes.

"Oh, that will take way too long," you say. *"If I go at that speed, it would take me a couple of years to quit smoking."*

Yes, it may take two years before you're completely off cigarettes, but if you add up the number of cigarettes you will smoke in the next two years and add up the number of cigarettes you would smoke in five, ten, or twenty years, which do you think is harder on your body and your wallet? Besides, that doesn't even take into account your frustration from failing to quit using conventional methods. There are methods that can get you to quit right now, but they probably won't last long. What is worse, after you relapse, you'll probably smoke more than you do now.

The best way to control your smoking is to control when you smoke. You can start by controlling the intervals between cigarettes, even if they are as short as fifteen minutes. But be consistent! If you want a cigarette after ten minutes, wait another five. Don't shorten your quit time. If fifteen minutes is too long, then

---

HELPER

What if you're on a schedule to smoke one cigarette every 15 minutes (that would be a little over three packs a day) and it's time to smoke, but you don't feel like it? Just wait until you feel like lighting up before starting your next 15-minute interval. You may decide that you can set your watch to go off at 16- or 17-minute intervals without any trouble. If you change from 15 to 16 minutes, try to stay at 16 minutes until you can lengthen the interval by another minute.

This is going to take some time, but imagine how you're going to feel when you are comfortable smoking every 24 minutes instead of every 15 minutes. At that point, you would be smoking two packs a day instead of three. Now *that's* progress.

SOMETHING TO THINK ABOUT

Let's do the math! If you're a three-pack-a-day smoker, you smoke almost 1,100 packs of cigarettes a year. That's almost 22,000 cigarettes. If you cut back to two packs a day, you'll smoke 7,300 fewer cigarettes a year.

You can go from 22,000 cigarettes a year down to zero. It's just going to take longer than it takes the person who starts out smoking half a pack a day. If you have a penny (which isn't much) and you double it every day, the second day you'd have two cents, the third day four cents, and so on. In twenty-eight days you'd be a millionaire. Now here's the hard part: What if you lost your million dollars, lost it all, and had to start all over? Would you give up? Or would you start over?

---

smoke every ten minutes. Start where you are comfortable and slowly stretch your quit time. No matter where you start, you will reach your goal.

Quitting on Schedule with a Twist

Everyone has special days, but the most personal day is usually your birthday. If you're quitting once an hour, then use your birth date to set your watch alarm. For example, if you were born on the tenth, then you would have a cigarette at ten minutes past each hour you are awake. Set your alarm to go off at ten minutes past the hour as a reminder to smoke. If you always light up as

---

ANOTHER HELPER

Look at what you can do, not at what you can't do. Unreasonable goals can't be met by anyone. And stop thinking about your sister-in-law! Just because she hasn't smoked for five years doesn't mean she is a stronger, wiser person. All it means is that she hasn't smoked for five years. Let it go! Now let's get back to you.

KEEP IN MIND

The alternatives to Quit Days really require a watch with an alarm or a timer. Be sure not to buy one with a really loud alarm or else you'll make everyone mad at you (and they might blow smoke in your face).

soon as you wake up, set your clock radio to wake you up a few minutes before the time you have a cigarette scheduled.

You don't have to use the day of your birthday—any number between one and fifty-nine is just as good—as long as the number means something special to you.

Having Quit Days or scheduling cigarettes is the easiest way to quit smoking you'll ever find. If and when you slip, you can quit when you're ready without feeling like a failure, without having to start all over again.

	ROADBLOCKS TO SUCCESS
Part 2	AND HOW TO GET
	AROUND THEM

6 | Roadblock #1— Other Smokers

Unless you live and travel where no one smokes, cigarettes are going to be in your life—sometimes a little, other times overwhelmingly so. You can smell cigarette smoke almost anywhere: on the sidewalk, in the parking lot, at a party, or through an open window. Your boss may smoke, your best friend may smoke, and there may be smokers in your family.

Sometimes you can't get away from cigarettes because you want the contract, you need directions, or you want to sell the car and the prospective buyers light up while you're talking. Maybe you can tell them that you'll talk outside so they don't smoke in your house, but you'll still be looking at and talking to people who are smoking.

Eventually, you'll automatically take steps to avoid cigarette smoke because you won't like it, but for now, you need a few strategies to keep the cigarettes from getting close.

Public Places Where People Are Smoking

Once you step outside, you can get a whiff of smoke when you're least expecting it, and it can be enough for you to make a beeline to the nearest store for cigarettes. Sometimes, that's all it takes.

When you're around smokers or you see a big ad showing a pack of cigarettes with several slender beauties reaching out the top of the open pack like dancers gliding down a flight of stairs, imagine how that's going to affect you in a weak moment! Those cigarettes are waiting for you when you walk inside the nearby convenience store to buy a quart of milk or a loaf of bread. The little battles you've been having inside your head are over, the case is closed, and you tell the clerk in a low voice, "and a pack of . . ."

On Your Quit Day

1. Stay away, as much as you can, from places where people generally smoke. And for heaven's sake, stay out of convenience stores! Your desire to smoke can increase or decrease depending on what's going on around you, where you are, and whom you're with. When you're face-to-face with a three-foot-high picture of a pack of cigarettes or you're around people lighting up after they leave the store, a cigarette can slide right in to home base.

2. When you see smokers on the sidewalk or wherever you happen to be, give them a wide berth. Try not to breathe their cigarette smoke, because when you're a new quitter, it will make you want to smoke. Later on, after you have been a quitter for a while, you won't like their smoke blowing in your face. If you practice avoiding smoke in public on smoking days as well as Quit Days, it will become second nature.

HELPER

If you see a cigarette in your hand, make it unattractive and unusable. Throw it away (legally and safely).

One quitter worked in public relations and several of his clients were smokers. On the night before his first few Quit Days, he took some cigarettes and splattered them with brewed coffee. His cigarettes were dry by the next morning, the beginning of his Quit Day, but they were stained and didn't look good. It was enough to prevent him from smoking around anyone, but he had the security of carrying his pack along wherever he went. When you take away the glamour and sex appeal the advertisers have associated with smoking, it loses many of its attractions. Make your cigarettes unattractive (but not unsanitary).

Smokers at Work—Coffee Breaks and Lunch

Being around people who smoke during coffee breaks and lunch is sometimes hard to avoid. Those rest periods from work are a pleasant time to socialize and relax. Trying to quit smoking using conventional methods means that every day you have to go off by yourself during lunch and breaks unless you're friends with non-smokers or quitters.

When you "Quit Before You Know It," you have the time and patience to find ways to enjoy your work breaks without having to be around cigarettes or smoke in your face. Here are a few suggestions:

Coffee Breaks

You only have a few minutes, but this is a crucial time to make a change because you have always stood outside with smokers. Try to refresh yourself so you'll feel better when you get back to work.

1. If there is a place where you can be by yourself or with a non-smoker, do some stretching exercises. They will make your body and brain feel more relaxed. There are some good books on stretching; also check the Internet. You can even sit and do some isometric exercises: you tense individual muscles, beginning with your forehead, and then let them relax. By the time you get down to your toes, your break will be half over and you'll feel a lot better than if you had stood outside and smoked.
2. Take the long way to get your beverage. If the coffee shop is across the street from where you work, or if you walk to a lunchroom or lunch wagon, walk to the corner and back before you get your coffee and snack.

    When Roy was a new quitter, he left the office on his coffee break and walked around the block before he stopped at Rosie's Diner for coffee and a bagel. He could have walked straight across the street from the office, but the extra walk pepped him up more than the coffee.

HELPER

It helps to start thinking like a nonsmoker. Ask yourself, *"What would I do if I couldn't stand the smell of cigarette smoke?"* Keep your answer in mind as you make decisions about how to deal with coffee breaks and lunches.

---

3. If you go outside, wave to the smokers, then keep walking. If you're friendly with any of them, be sure to explain to them beforehand that this is a Quit Day so they don't feel as though you're giving them a cold shoulder.
4. Check your bottled water supply, make sure you have some chewing gum or hard candy, stretch again, then return to work.

Lunch
Have a nice lunch you have either prepared or bought. Eat slowly and enjoy it.

1. Find a nonsmoking co-worker to talk to who doesn't sit with smokers. At first, you are going to have only one Quit Day a week, so this is the time to look for other nonsmokers or quitters. And look around—some people are reading instead of smoking, and some people are talking or walking and not smoking.
2. During the time when you would normally be smoking, put on some comfortable shoes and take a walk. If there's nothing outside except a parking lot, walk around the parking lot. Every step you take is a step in the right direction. Every walk, long or short, is nothing more than one step at a time. A few steps are better than no steps at all.
3. This is the time to work on the crossword puzzle. Eat a little lunch, take a short walk, then sit down and tackle the crossword puzzle. Buy a newspaper or bring one along. With the money you're saving by not smoking on your Quit Day, you can subscribe to a newspaper with a good crossword puzzle

and still have money left over. Make sure to save the puzzle for your Quit Day. Don't do it on days you smoke.

4. Read magazines and newspapers. Collect the ones you enjoy and save them for your Quit Day. Get an introductory subscription to a newspaper you don't usually read—a foreign newspaper can be very interesting. Some high-priced magazines have inexpensive subscription offers. Large bookstores offer a huge selection of magazines that are entertaining and informative.

5. Bring along an interesting book. Be sure your book is exciting; this isn't the time to read something dull. Travel books are good because they distract you from where you are and help you to "get out of yourself"—for a few minutes—which is all you need until lunch is over.

6. This is a good time to call a nonsmoking friend for a little support. When it was lunchtime, Julie called her friend Tracy, who told her to keep up the good work.

Lunch with the Group

It's your Quit Day. It is also Al the supervisor's birthday and everyone in your department is taking him out to lunch. Al smokes, so you'll be having lunch in a restaurant that allows smoking, and all the smokers you work with will be lighting up. Also, you will be taking extra time because, after all, Al is the boss; so lunch today is an hour and a half. There is plenty of time for smoking both before the first course and after the last crumbs of cake have been eaten. On such occasions, there are a few things you can do, and one thing you should definitely not do:

1. Try to find a seat that is away from where you think smoke will blow. This may or may not work because you don't know how the air will circulate. Your best chance to avoid smoke in your face is to have no one who smokes sitting on either side of you or across from you.

2. As soon as you can, ask for a glass of water with a twist of lemon. The lemon looks good and it keeps you busy. If you

prefer, have ice in the drink. Then concentrate on the menu. If everyone is getting a sandwich or salad, you should be served fairly quickly.

3. If you will be served a more elaborate meal than a sandwich, consider ordering a couple of appetizers instead of a heavy main course. This way, you'll have more variety in your meal and you will be busier with the food.

4. If there is bread, keep a piece in your smoking hand except when both hands are busy with your other food. You can hang on to the bread even after the main meal. If your co-workers remark about it, explain what you're doing. They will admire you. This is not the time to say you got the idea from someone else. Take all of the credit.

5. If there is dessert and coffee, you should have some if you wish. You have eaten modestly, not stuffed yourself, and you can finish off the meal with a sweet.

6. When people are smoking in the car on the way back to work, you will be stuck for a few minutes with smokers. Try to sit next to a nonsmoker and remember that lunch is almost over.

CAUTION!
If you have a cigarette, don't make the next day a Quit Day unless it has been scheduled. Don't suddenly change Quit Days. If you keep moving Quit Days around, you can arrange things so that you never have a Quit Day!

When Selling Cigarettes Is Part of Your Job

If you work at a market, liquor, or convenience store, you're handling packs of cigarettes throughout your shift. For someone who's been smoking for a while, that can be a tough one. If the basic plan is working well for you, then stick with it; but if you have too much trouble on Quit Days when you're at work, consider trying one of the alternative plans in chapter 5.

These plans have two advantages for you:

- First, you don't have to struggle through an entire Quit Day while you're facing smokers all day long.
- Second, although you'll be able to smoke from time to time each day, you are still quitting because you will slowly lengthen the time between cigarettes.

A difference between the alternative plans and the basic quit plan is that you will be structuring your quitting every day instead of once a week. But it's okay because *you're* going to decide how long you can go between cigarettes. Just be consistent and stick to your schedule. When you're sliding that cellophane package across the counter to a customer, you'll know that pretty soon you're going to have a cigarette.

If you are serious about quitting, you may want to consider looking for another job where you don't have to face temptation directly in the eye every day. I know that can take time, and it may not be possible right now. But look at it this way: in a few years will you regret having stayed at a job that prevented you from becoming a quitter?

SOMETHING TO THINK ABOUT

While you're making change or processing the customers' credit cards, do a little experiment. People who have smoked for several years, especially women, appear to age faster. If a woman has been smoking for fifteen or twenty years and her identical twin sister has never smoked, you can spot the smoker right away because she looks older, she has more wrinkles, and her skin shows greater damage. If someone new approaches you, try to predict if that person is going to ask you for a pack of cigarettes. You can't see it in the younger women, but it's obvious by the time they reach forty. This can liven up a boring day and show you firsthand what cigarettes are doing to your body.

If the Boss Smokes

When two people smoke together, it's a rite of friendship, of equality. Sometimes when the boss offers you a cigarette, it's a sign that you're about to be asked to take on more work.

Many buildings are now smoke-free, although if your boss smokes, chances are that you'll be breathing secondhand smoke. Carolyn, who works as an office temp, has worked in several "smoke-free" buildings with supervisors who smoked. She could have reported the violation to the city, but she wanted to work, so she put up with the smoke until she was able to move on. One supervisor told her, "I know you're not supposed to smoke here, but I smoke, and that's the way it is." Carolyn solved the problem by getting another job as soon as she could.

How you handle the situation depends on who is smoking, whether there is a smoke-free area where you can work, and how badly you need the job.

On Your Quit Day

1. If you have to work with someone who smokes, have your first several Quit Days on your days off. Eventually, though, you'll have a Quit Day around the smoker. By then, you may not want your good Quit Day efforts go up in smoke and you will be able to take some positive steps for your health and well-being.

2. See if there's any way to stay at your job and work where there isn't smoke. Try to put some distance between you and the smoker. If there is a smoke-free room or office, ask permission to use it on your Quit Days. Imagine what you would do if you had an illness such as asthma and you couldn't tolerate smoke. Imagine what your company would have to do to accommodate you.

3. The day may come when you decide it's time to choose between your work environment and your well-being. You have the right to take good care of yourself. Don't let others take that away from you.

   I know this can be difficult. Many people can't leave a job because of someone's smoking. Yet being unemployed is a short-

---

SOMETHING TO THINK ABOUT

If someone is the only smoker where she works, or if she moved to an area where smoking is frowned upon, do you think it would be easier for her to quit smoking? If you do, then can you see the effect your environment has on where, when, and how much you smoke.

---

term crisis, while the damage from smoking can lead to long-term problems.

4. You are entitled to a little courtesy. Be up front with both your boss and your co-workers. Tell them how hard you have struggled to quit and that you're finally succeeding. Most people will be considerate. But remember, there are some people who don't care if you're quitting or not. Don't let them get to you.

Friends Who Smoke

Longtime smokers who are quitting may find it especially difficult to be around friends who puff on cigarettes. If you have a social life that involves people who smoke and you need or want to be around them, plan your Quit Days carefully so you can enjoy their company. At the same time, your friends should go halfway to accommodate your desire to quit smoking.

Considerate friends will understand, and those are the people with whom you should socialize on Quit Days. Eventually, you'll probably spend most of your time socializing with nonsmokers or quitters.

HELPER

If you give your cigarettes to someone higher up on the food chain at work, every time you want to smoke, you'll have to ask Carlos the nonsmoking supervisor, for example, for a cigarette. That may reduce smoking pretty fast.

Before Your Quit Day

1. Make a list of nonsmokers and quitters you know and would like to be around. Think about ways to cultivate relationships with them on your Quit Days.

2. Think about activities you and your nonsmoking companions enjoy. Then make a list of activities to occupy you and your friends on your Quit Days. They should include some pleasant pastimes: dancing, singing, playing an instrument or listening to favorite music, going out to lunch or dinner, or cooking together. Plan to have one meal with a nonsmoking friend. Check the newspaper for movies, plays, concerts—whatever you and your friends enjoy that won't involve a lot of smokers.

On Your Quit Day

1. Talk to at least one good friend. If a friend supports your quitting, this is a good time to have a quick chat. Don't lean on the person, but a brief phone call can be a morale booster. Roy's friend Lily was usually available when he called for support. This helped him because he called her *before* he smoked, not after. But there will be a time when no one is around to talk to. That's okay, because you're getting along just fine.

2. Try something new. Take "safe" risks. If you have a skill you would like to pass on or if you'd like to learn something new, your Quit Day is the perfect time to try it out.

   Iris is an artist who offered painting lessons from her studio on her Quit Days to distract herself from craving cigarettes. An extra reward was that she began a part-time career as a painting teacher at the local university, which helped her to quit smoking.

   You have dreams and you have ideas. Try some of them out on your Quit Days. Don't become discouraged if the first two or three don't work out. Eventually, you'll find an activity that is right for you and will make you glad that you kept trying.

3. Use your success as a quitter to influence others. Iris didn't like to smoke around her students, and she didn't allow them

to smoke around her. As she became more involved in her teaching, Iris realized that her behavior strongly influenced the younger people. She knew that if she smoked, many of them would smoke, and she didn't want them to have to struggle for years as she had done before she went on the plan.

4. Follow through on those plans you have made with nonsmoking friends on your Quit Days! Sometimes you might want to light up and cancel the plans. It's okay to feel that way. Take a little time to relax and settle your thoughts; then go ahead with your plans to enjoy your day.

Relatives Who Smoke

You walk in the house and guess who's there? Your favorite relative has stopped by for a visit—but you could tell before you walked inside because of the clouds of smoke billowing from underneath the door.

How could Cousin Bette not be welcome in your home? How could you not invite her over for the holidays? You know that about thirty seconds after she walks in the front door, she'll sit down, look for an ashtray or saucer, and light up. And if it's twenty degrees outside and snowing, you can't send her outside to smoke. You may not be able to send her outside no matter what.

This is a touchy situation because feelings are going to be hurt—hers . . . or yours. You can allow people to tell you that you're being selfish and inconsiderate (and therefore let them have their way because things have always been like this), ask you why you are trying to break the family apart, and so on. You can do this, but you'll still be smoking.

On Your Quit Day

1. Try to arrange your first several Quit Days when you won't be seeing relatives who smoke. You have to be careful because if your dearly beloved aunt sighs and tells you that she wants to reward you by taking you to lunch—at a restaurant where she can smoke—you have to decide how you are going to handle

situations like this for the rest of your life. Now is the time for you to be an ex-smoker.

2. If you make plans with smokers, tell them how much you're looking forward to seeing them, but be sure to let them know that you're quitting smoking now and that they won't be able to smoke around you on your Quit Days.

   If smokers don't agree to abstain, you can see them another time. Don't let them use their smoking as a condition to maintain a relationship with you!

3. If smokers are guests in your home, ask them to smoke in another room by an open window or to go outside. If they don't like it, they can make the visit brief and smoke all they want after they leave. Smokers resent being bullied by nonsmokers, but quitters don't have to be bullied by smokers—even when they're family. The day will come when you won't want to be around people who smoke, and even beloved relatives will be told gently, but firmly, to smoke outside or somewhere else. If you give in to them "just this one time," they know you'll give in again.

   "But it's my Uncle Frank!"

   But they're *your* lungs; so don't put yourself in the way of overwhelming temptation. If you do it to "test your strength," you're setting yourself up for giving in, lighting up, and smoking. Give yourself a break!

   Ask for a little consideration because your decision to quit deserves respect. Don't let anyone beat you down by convincing you it's in the family's interest for you to smoke.

4. Don't fight about it. Becoming a quitter empowers you. Fighting gives it away. Sometimes it takes diplomacy and tact to get the respect you're entitled to.

5. Ask your relatives who smoke to help you. (They'll love that.) Say, "I need your help. I want to see you today, but I don't want to be tempted to smoke. Do you have any suggestions?" Then let them come up with ideas that will allow you to see each other without their smoking around you. Ask them for

their help, but don't make them responsible for your quitting. That's your job.

6. If family members refuse to be considerate, you have to decide how much control you want them to have over your life. That includes your health and well-being.

7. Relatives, as well as friends and even co-workers, frequently monitor quitters. Often, they're the first to point out that you're smoking and they feel obligated to remind you that it's your Quit Day. The following reply can be difficult, but try it out a few times. Say, *"Thank you."* Now, here's the really hard part but, believe it or not, it will make you feel good about yourself: let it go, and ignore further comments.

Using Bribes to Quit Smoking

Many quitters say they just need a good start—some way to keep from smoking for, say, a month or two, and then they can handle things on their own. In the spirit of being helpful, sometimes a relative will offer a payoff if the quitter doesn't smoke for a certain period of time. Bribes can work, but unfortunately only until the reward is given.

KEEP IN MIND

Of course, if you are a guest in a smoker's house, then you're the one who has to go outside when they're smoking. It would be great if they don't smoke around you, but if Christmas dinner is at Uncle Stan and Aunt Fran's this year, you can't tell them what to do. Find a smoke-free room in the house and escape when everyone starts lighting up, or go outside and take a walk. If the smokers won't help out, get together with relatives who don't smoke, or make the visits to inconsiderate relatives as brief as possible.

An exception is that if you're visiting relatives or friends to help them out and they want to light up, then they owe you consideration. They should not smoke until after you leave, and you have a right to tell them not to smoke.

There's a story that Joseph P. Kennedy promised his children a large sum of money (I think each child got a million bucks) if they wouldn't smoke until they were twenty-one. Since few people begin to smoke after that age, the offer was a wise one. And apparently it was effective because few, if any, of his nine children took up cigarettes.

If someone promises to give you a pile of money for not doing something you've never done anyway, the bribe may be a good incentive to keep you from starting. Otherwise, paying you off for quitting doesn't work because once you get the money, you have no reason not to resume smoking.

KEEP IN MIND

You cannot reinvent yourself in a day. Making drastic changes in order to become a quitter are usually temporary and the effects won't last. A good example of this would be to spend your savings (or take out a loan) on an expensive vacation to a "health" resort for a week or two where you aren't allowed to smoke. It's a great vacation if you can afford it, but in the long run it won't make you a quitter. This plan gives you the tools to quit smoking so that it fits naturally into your life.

Holidays and Special Occasions: A Reason to Put Off Quitting?

Holidays and special occasions can be stressful when you are busy and emotions are highly charged. You want to enjoy yourself as much as possible, which has usually meant setting self-improvement goals aside for a while. This is why many people put off quitting smoking until after the holidays.

An advantage of this plan is that you can "Quit Before You Know It" and still enjoy the company of family and friends, even if they smoke. If you have a special event planned, you can switch over to an alternative plan just for that day. When your next Quit Day comes around, revert to the original plan. You are still better off, however, if you can stick to a Quit Day through the celebration. You'll feel terrific and get a great boost to your self-confidence!

There will always be special days to celebrate with family and friends, some of whom *don't* smoke. Take your cues from them and spend as little time as possible around people who insist on smoking around you. Don't wait for a perfect time to quit smoking. If you put off quitting once, there's no reason why you can't put it off a thousand times.

HELPER

Delaying a cigarette for a while can help you delay a cigarette for a while longer. But when you vow to give up cigarettes forever, there isn't much point in delaying anything for an hour or two. One year is made up of 8,760 hours (or 8,784 hours if it's a leap year), which is a pretty long delay. When you're a new quitter, a short delay is much easier to handle because you can see a cigarette somewhere around the corner.

Achieving Long-Term Success

You'll be more likely to achieve long-term success as a quitter if your family members, friends, and co-workers don't smoke. The influence of other smokers makes quitting more difficult. But the more confidence you have in your ability to stay off cigarettes, the easier it will be to ask them not to smoke around you. As your Quit Days add up, so will your good feelings.

SUMMARY: ROADBLOCK #1—OTHER SMOKERS
Public Places Where People Are Smoking
- Avoid places where you'll see people smoking.
- If you see smokers, move away from them.

Smokers at Work
Coffee Breaks
- S-T-R-E—T——C——H and take a short walk away from smokers.
- Check your chewing gum, water, and hard candy supplies.
- Don't make a beeline to get your coffee; take the long way.

Lunch
- Find a nonsmoking co-worker to talk to who doesn't sit with smokers.
- Take a walk.
- Do a crossword puzzle.
- Read magazines or a book you have saved for Quit Days.
- Call a nonsmoking friend for a little support.

Lunch in a Restaurant with Smokers
- Sit between and across from nonsmokers.
- Ask for a glass of water with a twist of lemon as soon as you are seated. Concentrate on your beverage and the menu.
- Order appetizers instead of an entrée.
- Keep a piece of bread in your smoking hand.
- Try not to sit next to a smoker in the car when returning to work.

When Selling Cigarettes Is Part of Your Job
- An alternative plan might be best. You can smoke on schedule while cutting down every day.
- Look for another job where you don't have to face temptation.

Working with Smokers
- Schedule your first few Quit Days on your day off.
- Work away from smokers. You're entitled to this courtesy.
- If you can't get away from smoke, look for another job.

Friends Who Smoke

- Ask friends who smoke not to smoke around you. Or plan your Quit Days carefully if certain friends continue to smoke around you and you still want to spend time with them.
- Cultivate relationships with nonsmokers or quitters. Find activities both of you enjoy. Then follow through on your plans to get together.
- Talk to at least one nonsmoking friend for support when you're tempted to smoke.
- Use your success as a quitter to influence others.

Relatives Who Smoke

- Try to arrange your first several Quit Days when you won't be seeing relatives who smoke.
- Don't let others pressure you to smoke; stick to your decision to quit.
- Don't fight about it. Becoming a quitter empowers you.
- Ask relatives who smoke to help you find ways to be together without smoking.
- Ignore the comments of relatives who try to monitor you, and don't let them bribe you to smoke or to quit.

7 | Roadblock #2— Living with a Smoker

Quitting is more difficult if you live with someone who isn't ready to quit. There have been quit groups for couples, but they have met with mixed success. One of the main problems is that quitting turns into a competition between the partners, and that can spell trouble. If your husband, wife, partner, or roommate has no interest in your quitting smoking, even though your relationship is good, your efforts to quit may cause stress, and quitting will be more difficult. Following a few simple guidelines can make all the difference; you can be a successful quitter without harming your relationship.

Before Your Quit Day
1. Cooperation is the key to success. Make written agreements. Quitting on this plan is so gradual, it is the best way for both you and your partner to become accustomed to your quitting. But while you're going it alone, some of your success as a quitter depends upon your partner's cooperation. Talk things over with him or her and make a list of what both of you are willing to do and not do. Write it down so there isn't any misunderstanding.
2. With your partner, make a list of rewards for the partner's co-operation (although there can be some surprises!).
   There are all kinds of rewards to make things interesting, from taking over one of the partner's usual chores, to special sex, to having a night out. (Don't ever withhold sex to punish your partner.)
3. Purge cigarettes and smoking paraphernalia from your common

living areas the night before your Quit Day. Ask your partner to keep his or her smoking things put away.

4. Plan your Quit Days so that they don't conflict with your partner's smoking.

Don't schedule your first few Quit Days when you're spending most of the day with your partner. If you both work outside the home, choose a Quit Day during the workweek.

5. Your partner needs to have a separate to place to smoke. Having a "smoking room" in the house on your Quit Day can save your Quit Day. One couple telephoned each other from different parts of the house and had long conversations. When the weather is good, it's especially considerate if the smoker goes outside to smoke.

If you live in a small apartment with absolutely no place for the partner to smoke away from you, be prepared to do some troubleshooting and compromising. Since you share your home, the smoker has a right to be relaxed and do the normal activities that both of you did before you quit smoking. In a situation like this, you need to plan your first few Quit Days when you won't see much of your partner. In return, your partner should not smoke inside the apartment.

Sooner than you think, you're going to find the smell of cigarette smoke unpleasant. Take some time now to decide what compromises both of you are willing to make to accommodate one person's smoking while the other person remains a quitter.

On Your Quit Day

1. Avoid disrupting the household with your quitting.

The plan outlined here is ideal for someone living with a smoker who isn't ready to become a quitter, because when you quit smoking only one day a week, it will hardly cause a ripple in the household. When you get up to two days a week, your partner will begin to realize that this time you might be onto something that's working.

Bob planned his first few Quit Days for the days when he was at school until three o'clock, and then he coached baseball until dinner. As a reminder to himself, he used math as a teaching tool by having his students calculate the time left when he would technically be able to light up again (if he were awake at midnight). When he got home, he spent the evening with his wife, Ellen, and the children. Ellen had agreed not to smoke in front of him, so Bob's Quit Days were busy and successful.

2. Avoid competition.

When the smoking partner sees that the quitter is succeeding, competition can come into play. Without thinking, a partner can interfere with the quitter's success, and do it in small ways that can nevertheless make a big difference—such as leaving their agreed-upon smoking room with a cigarette or keeping the door open while a cigarette is burning. Be understanding about these slips; usually they are unintentional.

3. Quitting is *your* responsibility.

Don't ask a partner or roommate to hold your cigarettes for you. Involving them in your self-control efforts is a sure way to put stress on a relationship, no matter how good it is. Quitting smoking is *your* job.

4. You need a supportive partner, not a supervisor or guard.

Some of the people we know, like, or love can unintentionally sabotage our efforts for self-improvement. Your partner may try to reassure you when you slip by saying something like, "That's okay, sweetie, it takes a lot of strength to quit smoking, and not everybody has it." Ouch!

All you need is cooperation, not monitoring. If he or she says, "Isn't this a Quit Day for you?" ask the other person, gently, gently, to please not pay attention to your smoking or quitting. (It's bad when the partner catches you smoking and remarks on it, and it's just as bad when the partner points out how "good" you're being when you don't smoke.)

How a Smoker You Live With Can Help You Out

- Ask the smoker to close the door to the designated "smoking room" so there is as little tobacco odor in the house as possible. If the phone rings and it's outside the smoking room, the smoker should put out the cigarette before leaving the room.

- Ask the smoker to keep cigarettes, lighter, ashtray, and so on, out of sight. It's too tempting for you to see them.
- The smoker should not ask you to pick up cigarettes if you're going out. That's too tempting.
- The smoker should not play with a lighter or carry cigarettes outside of the smoking room.
- Ask the smoker not to call attention to any "slips" you have on a Quit Day or point out that you're "being good." People who monitor your smoking place themselves in a position of superiority to you, which, of course, is incorrect.

This may seem like a list of petty dos and don'ts; but they can be a tremendous help on Quit Days. And you should thank the people you live with profusely for helping out.

KEEP IN MIND

If your house smells like cigarettes, you're going to have a harder time quitting. If your partner smells like cigarettes, whether or not you smell smoke in the house, it could be a cue for you to smoke. You're living with someone you care for, so keep in mind that you will be at greater risk for relapse. When you're off cigarettes for weeks or months, your partner will probably become a quitter. Meanwhile, this plan is the best way to quit if you live with a smoker.

SUMMARY: ROADBLOCK #2—LIVING WITH A SMOKER
Before Your Quit Day

- Make written agreements. Decide what each of you is willing to do and not do.
- With your partner, make a list of rewards for the partner's cooperation (you can plan some surprises!).
- Remove cigarettes and smoking items from living areas you share.

- Plan your first few Quit Days so that they don't conflict with your partner's smoking.
- Have a smoking room for your partner with the door closed. And stay out.

On Your Quit Day
- Avoid disrupting the household with your quitting.
- Avoid competition.
- Remember that quitting is *your* responsibility.

How a Smoker You Live With Can Help You Out
- Ask the smoker to close the door to the smoking room.
- Ask the smoker to keep all smoking items out of sight.
- The smoker should not ask you to buy cigarettes.
- The smoker should not play with a lighter or carry cigarettes outside the smoking room.
- Ask the smoker not to call attention to any Quit Day "slips" or point out that you're "being good." You need a supportive partner, not a supervisor.

8 Roadblock #3— The Three Jitters: Anxiety, Worry, and Stress

When you're worried and the stress level is high, the first thing that comes to mind is, *"I need a cigarette."*

It's a comfort to light up and take a quick nicotine hit. And it's so easy! You don't need a prescription from the doctor; you don't need a shoulder to cry on. Cigarettes are there for you in a crisis, and they are a quick, but temporary, fix for the jitters.

Any combination of the three jitters—anxiety, worry, and stress—can give you a little tap on the arm, and self-control can fly out the window in an instant. Many people have resumed smoking after a personal crisis—divorce, job loss, or nothing more than having the filling of a sandwich fall down their front just before an important meeting.

Stress can be big and deep, or it can be a temporary pain in the neck. People who haven't smoked in years can have one bad moment and mutter, "I've had it." Then off they go to buy or "borrow" cigarettes. It doesn't fix the dent in the fender or recover the lost promotion, but if you smoked in stressful situations before, there is *no* guarantee that you won't turn to cigarettes when stress strikes again.

Why Cigarettes Give Temporary Relief

Nicotine is a psychoactive drug that gives people a sense of well-being; it's similar to the effects ethanol has on alcoholic drinks or opiates have on narcotics. That's why you feel better almost immediately after you light up. At the same time, nicotine is a stimulant that gives you extra energy. That's the odd and seductive thing about cigarettes: they both energize and relax you. Trying to put that in your past, trying to give it up "forever," is hard to do if your rent just got raised, or your brother-in-law still hasn't found a job and he'll be camping on your sofa for at least ten more years.

But he has cigarettes.

Why Smoking Doesn't Help

There's a huge downside to this. If you're anxious, a cigarette won't relieve your anxiety; if you're tense, a cigarette won't help you to relax. The "hit" is so brief that you have to keep puffing, and the more you puff, the more you have to puff, because all those drugs in tobacco increase anxiety. It's like having a drink to help a hangover. You take in more of what's hurting you because that's your way to get fast relief.

Smoking is one of the worst things you can do to relieve anxiety or stress, because cigarettes constrict the blood vessels and make you more tense. That's why high blood pressure is called *hyper*tension. If you've been smoking for several years, your blood pressure is probably elevated; and if you have anxiety or panic attacks, getting off cigarettes should be a priority.

Anxiety and Panic Attacks

Anxiety and panic attacks are on the same continuum except panic attacks are worse. To describe panic attacks to my students, I ask them to imagine that they're strapped into a spaceship, alone, and the ship has gone out of orbit and is heading into deep space. They look out at the stars and the darkness of infinity as they head farther and farther away from Earth. There will be no rescue, of course. That is the terrifying loneliness of a panic attack. Every time I've described panic attacks, someone has waited after class and thanked me for helping them know that they aren't alone.

If you've had trouble quitting smoking because you sometimes become anxious, nervous, or even have panic attacks, this plan will help you to avoid them. Let the plan do the work for you while you relax, and you will quit smoking before you know it.

On Your Quit Day

1. Keep in mind that on this plan, you don't need to worry about the stress from quitting. When you quit today, and your cigarettes are just around the corner tomorrow, that stress just isn't there. If you can't last for an entire day, have just one cigarette an hour for several days until you can quit for an entire day. (See chapter 5, "Alternative Plans.")

2. Don't fill your Quit Days with chores. If you have a lot of chores lined up, you'll need a little break from all that work, and it will be all too easy to reach for a smoke.

   Many quitters try to distract themselves by keeping busy with the things they usually do every day anyway. That isn't going to do you any good. While you're mopping the floor or trying to read the quarterly report, you may see nothing except a cigarette, a lighter, an ashtray, and you.

3. Except for emergencies, make your Quit Days something to look forward to. Save what you like best for Quit Days as much as possible.

4. Experiment with ways to stay away from a cigarette that don't cause you stress. Your backup is always "I can smoke tomorrow."

5. Stay away from the smoking police. They cause stress and they contribute to relapse.

   Are any of these comments familiar?

   - "I thought you quit smoking."
   - "I'm going to go and have a cigarette; I'd invite you to come outside with me, but I don't want to tempt you."
   - "I've never smoked. I wouldn't do that to myself."

Comments like these can make your stomach churn. But you should feel good about yourself because you didn't make them. If someone points out what they see as your shortcomings, it's best to say nothing and let the words float away. It can also be very helpful if you take a few moments to imagine what a person you admire would say or do in the same situation. Having an imaginary role model—even if you know that person never smoked—can show you a way to cope while, at the same time, allow you to feel good about what you're doing.

There's a fine line between having people support you and having them upset you. It's one thing to ask you how you're doing, but expressions of concern are irritating. You didn't just have major surgery, so tell everyone to lighten up. Nicely.

6. The best thing for stress is the "medicine" that clears your head: physical exercise. Move around if you can. Burn up a little of that extra energy on something good for yourself.

I know that many of you can't get to a swimming pool—and you shouldn't exercise beyond a good walk without your doctor's okay—but swimming almost always makes me feel really good, no matter what has been on my mind. And if you think I'm an athlete, think again. There isn't one athletic gene in my body, but I have plenty of couch genes and a lot more from the potato family. Exercise relieves stress for everyone who gets the body moving.

7. If you're upset, call a friend, talk it over with your dog or cat (you're supposed to do that, anyway), or have a good cry. A cigarette won't make you feel better, but good friends will. Cats and dogs are good listeners, and unlike therapists, they don't charge you a lot of money.

8. Discover something you love. For Carolyn, a single mother who was laid off from her last two jobs, it was Raphael's painting of Pope Julius II.

Although Carolyn was always stressed out over money, she kept searching for a way to relieve her anxiety. Finally, she took a step she had been thinking about for the past few years. As she got older she didn't feel as though she would fit in if she returned to school (she was thirty-one at the time). But she became desperate enough to risk failure, or as she said, "make

> **SOMETHING TO THINK ABOUT**
>
> There is an excellent little book called *How to Get Control of Your Time and Your Life* by Alan Lakein in which the author tells the reader how to get things done and to reach goals. For someone stuck in the worry track the book is very helpful. I made the book required reading in my behavior management classes. First published in 1974, the paperback has been reprinted more than fifty times and it's still in print.

a fool of myself." Because she had always loved art, she registered for a painting class at the local university.

When Carolyn heard how Iris, her art teacher, was quitting smoking by using the plan, she figured that if someone who had been smoking for over forty years could quit, she could too. By taking a chance and going back to school, Carolyn discovered both art history and the plan, which helped her to finally quit smoking. Carolyn was busier than ever with scrambling for work, taking care of her son, and going to school, but she was happier than she had been in a long time. Although she had reasons to feel stressed out, Carolyn was able to handle stress more easily, and do it without a cigarette.

Relax!

You'll reduce the jitters when you relax. Here are some old standards as well as a couple of new ones:

- Close your eyes and take several slow, deep breaths. Sound silly? Try it for yourself.
- Imagine that the person of your dreams (you don't have to tell anyone who it is) has just walked up to you and is nuzzling your neck.
- Picture people who have particularly intimidated you wearing

tall, pointy hats with elastic bands under their chins to hold them up. It's very useful if you do this with snobby people you come in contact with. Try it the next time you see one of them.

• Try a relaxation or meditation tape or CD. The idea may seem strange at first, but many successful people rely on it as a way to relieve stress. Follow the instructions on the tape or CD and do your meditation or relaxation exercises only on Quit Days. That way, you'll have something to look forward to. Make your Quit Days as enjoyable and relaxing as you can.

There are a lot of tapes and CDs available on relaxation, but not all of them are good. Ask around for recommendations or, if possible, listen to one before you buy it. Your local library may be a good place to look. You may have to try a few before you find something you love enough to take into your bedroom.

• If there's a yoga class in your area, give it a try. Relaxation can be a combination of yoga, deep breathing, or different types of meditation. Hatha yoga is quiet and nonstressful, but it can give you a wonderful workout. You do the positions that make you comfortable, and rest on your mat during the ones you don't feel like doing.

Relaxation techniques are easy to master and they're better than popping Valium or Xanax, or having the TV going constantly in the background. Relaxation is a tool that gives you

---

SOMETHING TO THINK ABOUT

Daniel Goleman has some relaxation recordings on the market that are very good. *The Art of Meditation* describes four different relaxation techniques. One of them, the "body scan," takes about fifteen to twenty minutes, and it's time well spent, no matter how busy you are. Using principles of isometric squeeze relaxation (also known as progressive relaxation), Goleman leads you through a series of very relaxing exercises. The recording I've listened to is so good, I've never heard the end of it!

greater control over your life. It's a survival skill, and the more survival skills you have, the better you'll be able to deal with anxiety, stress, and worry. Using these relaxation techniques on your Quit Days may leave you more relaxed than on your smoking days!

KEEP IN MIND

Worry, stress, and anxiety will always be with us, but they aren't the three Fates. You can take steps to reduce them when they come calling. The more you can control these unpleasant emotions, the more likely you are to have a fulfilling life.

SUMMARY: ROADBLOCK #3—THE THREE JITTERS: ANXIETY, WORRY, AND STRESS

On Your Quit Day

- Keep in mind that on this plan you don't need to relieve the stress from quitting because, for now, quitting is not forever.
- Try to avoid unpleasant chores on your Quit Day or keep them to a minimum.
- Make Quit Days something to look forward to. Save what you like best for them as much as possible.
- Experiment with ways to stay away from cigarettes.
- Stay away from the smoking police.
- Move that body! The best thing for stress is physical exercise.
- Talk to a friend: a person, or your dog or cat.
- Give gentle yoga a try.
- Use some of the relaxation suggestions, including listening to tapes or CDs.

9 | Roadblock #4—Boredom

Life is filled with downtime: waiting for the coffee to be made, the traffic to move, the kids to get out of school, the bus to come, the phone to ring, the show to start, the washer to finish, the clothes to dry, the kettle to boil, the workday to end, the cows to come home.

Smoking is very handy when you're bored: the nicotine keeps you awake, and the cigarette keeps you busy.

This can be useful in a variety of settings. Perhaps you have a job where you have almost no work but are allowed to smoke. Or you are routinely stuck in traffic or spend hours watching your kids play in baseball tournaments over the summer. When time drags on and the day seems excruciatingly dull, smoking can make you feel like you're busy. You don't realize how much empty space smoking fills until you quit.

When You're Bored at Home
When you're at home, one of the greatest escapes from boredom is the remote control. With that little gadget you don't even have to get off the sofa to surf the hundred-plus channels. Sometimes, the only diversion is the little nicotine lift you get every few minutes from a cigarette.

On Your Quit Day
1. If you always smoke when you're watching TV, choose a Quit Day on which you don't watch much TV, or watch it with a nonsmoking friend who doesn't like smoke.

2. Turn off the television and do something new on your Quit Day—nothing drastic, just a little change. If you eat cornflakes every morning for breakfast, try something different: yogurt, fresh fruit, and a slice of bread from the good bakery you finally visited. Or wear a really snappy outfit to work or that outlandish tie no one has seen. Read the *New York Review of Books* or the *New York Times Book Review* and find some interesting new books. Sample at least one new activity on your Quit Day, and remember that a sample isn't the same as a purchase. You'll never know if you like something until you try it out.

3. Look in the Yellow Pages for health clubs or the YMCA and see how far one of them is from where you live. Is it within walking or driving distance? If so, call and ask for a tour of the facility. You don't have to join, just look. Tell them you're trying to stop smoking and you'd like to know what equipment or programs they have that might be good for you. That's all. After the tour, say *"Thanks,"* and go home. Then think about having a place where you could go almost any time you feel like it and where you could do a little or a lot. Just think it over.

    Experimenting with new things doesn't mean you're committed to them for life. Trying things on doesn't mean you have to buy them. But sometimes you can discover something you love.

4. "Kill time" productively. There's a good reason to try something new when you have a few minutes or more on your hands. Sometimes you really *do* find a new activity you enjoy. Following are some suggestions for killing time on your Quit Days. While you're doing any of these activities, smoking is either inconvenient, not allowed, or difficult to do at the same time. That doesn't mean you aren't able to take a cigarette break, but the activity itself would be difficult to do if you were smoking. If you're counting minutes until you can have a cigarette, killing time and enjoying yourself for a few minutes will make you happier.

> **HELPER**
> *Watch Time Pass on Your Quit Day*
> Every day has 1,440 minutes. Every day has 86,400 seconds (plus a few nanoseconds, but let's not quibble). When the minutes or the seconds get down to zero, the Quit Day is over. In your spare time, count down the minutes and seconds left until midnight.
> If you count down, you can see for yourself that the results keep changing. The day really isn't endless, the Quit Day is going to end, and before long you're going to smoke. If you distract yourself for even a few minutes and then recount the minutes remaining until you can smoke, you'll see that time is running out.

On the other hand, there are activities that accommodate smoking: listening to the music, waiting for the fish to bite, talking on the phone. On Quit Days, avoid doing what has always led you to a cigarette.

When You're Stuck in a Boring Situation
Let's get back to Carolyn for a moment, who is sitting at her desk. She has to be there for almost eight hours, she has little work to do, and she can't get up and walk around because she's supposed to be at her desk. She has very few options. She isn't allowed to have a book on her desk because that would look unprofessional. She has to sit and do nothing. That way, everyone except Carolyn is happy.

On Your Quit Day
Here are some suggestions to relieve the boredom from endless sitting or standing around:

1. Keep lists of skills and subjects you want to learn. When you have time to kill, review your lists, add to them, and make plans.
2. Use the computer if you have access to one. Play a game such as solitaire or chess.

3. Play with a small (and quiet) puzzle. There are all kinds of puzzles, from easy to brain-crunching, in little books you can find at most bookstores. There are very small computers with puzzles on them now, and it's worth investing a few bucks to buy one to pass the time. An Internet site called "Sliding Block Puzzles" will keep you entertained for days: visit www.johnrausch.com/SlidingBlockPuzzles/. You can also look at a search engine under "puzzles," including online crossword puzzles.
4. Get in the habit of carrying a small paperback book with you.
5. Begin writing that story! You know, the one you talked about the other day and the other person said, "That would make a good story." Has there ever been a better time?
6. Contact schools or colleges that interest you and get two course catalogs from each. Tear the pages out of one of the catalogs; put some of them in your pockets and read about the college and the courses you'd like to take. The other course catalog you keep at home, intact.

KEEP IN MIND

When you get outside for your break or lunch, you may want to light up. But you know what happens after that nicotine rush. It's all downhill, and smoking at break will make your afternoon worse. Remember, you have to return to that workstation or desk. Try not to plan Quit Days for days when you have a lot of downtime, although sometimes it's unavoidable.

Last Words on Boredom

Everybody gets bored. All of us have time on our hands. Think of all those times when you have said, *"I'd love to do that if I had the time . . ."* In fact, you really do have the time; it's just chopped up into chunks throughout the day. Some of those things you think you don't have time for can be parceled out into small enough increments so that you can get them done. Dealing with boredom is an art.

Here are some ideas to try on a Quit Day:

- Make vacation plans with the money you're saving by not smoking.
- Paint, draw, or cut out paper hearts. Go to an art supply store, buy paper, lettering, and trimming, and make your own valentines, birthday, and holiday cards.
- Get a Nerf ball and a hoop. Put it in your office or room where you watch TV.
- Buy origami paper and learn how to fold it.
- Shop for a new Rolls-Royce. Can't afford it? So what?
- Play the piano or the guitar, fiddle around, or take lessons.
- Have sex.
- Type. It keeps your hands busy. Make your own Web site.
- Learn to play the mandolin or the clarinet.
- Saw, hammer, drill. Build something.
- Learn a foreign language from a nonsmoker.
- Do yoga; meditate.
- Plan a trip to your ancestors' homeland.
- Get involved in a literacy program for adults or children.
- Coach a team, lead a troop, tutor kids, teach a skill.
- Take a class making stained glass. Take a class in anything. (Don't hang out with the smokers.)
- Volunteer to be a visitor at a hospital.
- Volunteer at your local Audubon Society; go birding. Volunteer at the zoo or humane society.
- Visit nonsmoking friends or call a quitter.
- Fly a kite.
- Get involved in local politics. Be a volunteer worker for your party.
- Take up bridge, hearts, or canasta (with nonsmokers).
- Support your local museum, ballet, or orchestra. Get involved!

- Join your local food co-op (the members usually don't smoke cigarettes).
- Go to your local chess club and learn the game (unless smoking is allowed).
- Sew, learn needlepoint, crochet, do embroidery.
- Take a knitting class or knit at your local yarn shop. (Men knit too!)

Summary: Roadblock #4—Boredom

On Your Quit Day (When You're at Home)
- Turn off the television and stay busy. Most of your activities should be enjoyable.
- Check out your local health club.
- "Kill time" by doing things where you can't smoke or smoking is inconvenient.
- Try one new activity.
- Get together with a nonsmoker and do something both of you like.
- If you watch TV, watch with someone who doesn't like cigarette smoke.

On Your Quit Day (When You're Stuck in a Boring Situation)
- Keep lists of skills and subjects you want to learn.
- Play a game on the computer. Look up puzzle sites on the Internet.
- Keep a small handheld computer game or puzzle with you.
- Carry small paperback books with you.
- Begin writing that story!
- Get course catalogs from a college you'd like to attend.

10 | Roadblock #5—Just Out of Bed in the Morning and Just Before Bed at Night

Just Out of Bed

What do you do as soon as you wake up in the morning? Well, okay; but after that, what do you do?

The best cigarette of the day is the first, and going without that morning cigarette can seem like walking the plank with nothing beneath it except the cold, deep, gray ocean. And then . . . nothing; and off you go. That's what getting out of bed and facing the day without a cigarette is like for someone who has vowed to quit "forever." But for someone who is going to quit for only a day, although it isn't always a tiptoe through the tulips, it can be done without pain and suffering.

In order to meet this challenge successfully, you have to plan ahead because when you face the day without a cigarette, there's an emptiness in you, a longing for something—gee whiz! It's a need. You haven't smoked in hours, and you're in nicotine withdrawal.

You need to make plans *before* your Quit Day.

The Night Before Your Quit Day

1. Get all cigarettes out of the house. Put away all smoking paraphernalia: lighters, matches, ashtrays, and anything else you use for smoking. Smoke your last cigarette, get rid of any cigarettes, and wash the ashtray after safely disposing the cold butts and ashes. Don't leave this for tomorrow morning!

   If you live with a smoker, this is where his or her cooperation is crucial. You can't ask the other person to quit with you, but you need some help with this. Make sure that the smokers in the house keep their smoking supplies out of sight. Also, you should remove any of your belongings you'll need during your Quit Day from the designated smoking room or area so you don't have to "run in for just a moment" to get something.

2. Get the coffee ready. You want your morning coffee or tea ready to plug in or prepare the minute you get out of bed. You have to get things going quickly on the morning of your Quit Day so you don't have time to think. Thinking too much on a Quit Day sometimes isn't good.

On Your Quit Day

1. Because you don't have cigarettes, and the smokers you live with have carefully put away theirs, the only way you can smoke as soon as you wake up is to run outside real fast in your jams and find cigarettes. No matter what, you can't get a cigarette right away. This is very important!

   If you live with someone who is lighting up in the house, be firm—it's your Quit Day. Ask for a little consideration. You may have to make a deal. That's okay. If the smoker doesn't pay any of the household expenses, you don't have to make a deal. No smoking in the house.

2. Plug in the coffee pot, or pour a cup that has been timed to be ready. (Plan to have the coffee ready as soon as you get up or step out of the shower.)

3. Hop into the shower. Now you're naked and it probably wouldn't be right for you to run outside until you put some clothes on (although it might liven up your neighbors' day).

4. You're doing great! Now for the next steps:

   a. Clothes (now or later)
   b. Coffee
   c. Dance (also, orchestra conducting if you're playing music)
   d. Breakfast
   e. Brush teeth

Drink some coffee, eat a little breakfast, dance the bossa nova (this is a requirement!), get dressed, and brush your teeth—which are thanking you down to their little roots for not smoking.

5. Leave, if you must. If there is a smoker in the house who is being difficult, or if you just want to get out, go to a nonsmoking café for a cappuccino. (Your spouse may be quite surprised to see that you really mean what you're saying and maybe *next* time will respect your Quit Day and not smoke in the house.)

   If you have children, take them out to breakfast. What an idea! Go to a restaurant before school, and you can have coffee. If you're a single parent and can't afford to buy cappuccinos for the kids (just kidding), then pack food and juice and go to the park. Joan bundles up her children when the weather is bad and they go over to a nonsmoking friend's apartment for breakfast. Joan takes along a loaf of cinnamon bread, and she and her friend Lois make french toast. The children love it, and Joan gets off to a good start on her Quit Day.

6. Get busy. Get on with your life and remember: you're going to have a cigarette in a few hours! Tomorrow you'll smoke with your morning coffee.

KEEP IN MIND

Make your Quit Day a good health day when it comes to eating. French toast is better when it's either baked or cooked with a small amount of canola oil. Don't go overboard in the other direction, either. Quitting smoking isn't about food, so don't change your eating patterns on Quit Days except to make the food attractive and tasty.

Don't say, *"It's my Quit Day, so I deserve a reward,"* as you head off for breakfast at the donut shop. You *do* deserve rewards on your Quit Day, in fact, lots of them, but indulge in other ways. You're quitting smoking for one day. Save the donuts for tomorrow if you have to have them.

Before Bed

Most smokers feel that they need a cigarette to cap off the day, even though nicotine actually keeps them awake longer. This is a time when some new quitters have second thoughts. What happened to Roy is typical.

Second Thoughts on Quit Night

Roy went through a Quit Day without smoking, but in the evening he began to have second thoughts. He called his nonsmoking friend Lily for support, but she didn't have time to talk. Roy had run out of things to do and he was getting edgy. He calculated the nanoseconds left until midnight, which was a little over five hours. Roy had waited this long and there wasn't that much time to go, but he was wondering if it was worth it. Maybe he should just quit cold turkey or join another group. Maybe this time it would work. But then he remembered that it hadn't worked before. But maybe it would work this time if he really tried. That was it! Roy hadn't tried hard enough!

He decided that he had three choices: he could try cold turkey again, he could keep smoking and forget about quitting, or he could continue using the plan. If he decided to go cold turkey, he couldn't have a cigarette tomorrow morning.

Could he do that? The answer was absolute: No. He wanted a cigarette as soon as possible, and that left him with the choice of lighting up right now or lighting up in the morning. He decided that quitting was still important and he could last for another few hours. *But he couldn't last any longer!*

Roy made a snack, something he'd suddenly decided he'd do on Quit Days. He watched a movie, chewed gum, and listened to modern jazz—all at the same time. His Quit Day was coming to a close and Roy turned in a little early.

1. If you have a partner, give each other a massage.

   Bob and Ellen took a massage class after he became serious about quitting, and instead of having the "last cigarette" together before they go to bed, they give each other a massage while talking about their day. It has been a terrific substitute for a cigarette and has added a little extra pizzazz to their relationship.

2. If you don't have a massage therapist, listen to a relaxation tape or CD. If you're restless and thinking that maybe, just maybe, you could throw on some clothes and run to the store, this is the time to turn to the relaxation exercises. Make sure to do this only on Quit Nights. Relaxation is a better way to end your day than smoking an eye-watering, throat-burning cigarette. Even if you're lying next to someone, you can put in earplugs and listen to the tape or CD. By the time it ends you'll be sleeping.

3. You could end your day with a little gentle yoga. Not only is it good for stress, but it also improves sleep.

   Yoga is an extremely useful series of stretching exercises that will keep you limber long into old age. Think of it as a tool to extend or even renew some of the physical ease you had when you were younger. Some of the positions are truly mind-boggling, but some of the easy positions can be handled by almost anyone.

   If you lie down on the floor, preferably on a mat on the carpet, you can do three or four of the easy poses before you go to bed. There are many books and videos about yoga, but stick to the easy poses for now. If you find that you really enjoy yoga, sign up for a class to learn more.

4. A few good stretching exercises can make you feel terrific. Don't worry; they don't have to be yoga stretches—the ones you remember from gym class will do wonders too.

SOMETHING TO THINK ABOUT

If you read a book on your first few Quit Nights, make sure it's a page-turner. Your mind may begin to wander, and a wandering mind isn't a good thing when you're trying to get through the evening without a cigarette.

5. Have the snack you planned *in advance* for your Quit Night. A little healthy treat is okay on your first few Quit Nights. Have something ready to go: a carton of low-fat yogurt and some strawberries sounds good, doesn't it? Or how about a thin slice of low-fat cheese and some nice mustard on a slice of bread? Plan ahead for the snack so you don't eat the frozen waffles.

6. Floss and brush your teeth with fancy toothpaste. Only on Quit Mornings and Nights should you use the really expensive stuff. Some of the best is from Italy or France, and it's so decadent you wouldn't dream of smoking after you brush your teeth with it. When you're through brushing, put the toothpaste away for your next Quit Day.

7. You made it! Now go to bed. You're having a cigarette in a few hours.

Summary: Roadblock #5—Just Out of Bed in the Morning and Just Before Bed at Night

The Night Before Your Quit Day

- Get all cigarettes out of the house.
- Get the coffee ready so you don't have to spend time making it in the morning.

On Your Quit Day

- No one is allowed to smoke in the house (except in a designated smoking room with the door closed).
- Plug in the coffee pot, or pour a cup that has been timed to be ready as soon as you get up or hop out of the shower.
- Take a shower.
- Eat a nourishing breakfast that you like—even if it's just a piece of fruit.
- Dance.
- If you want, go to a nonsmoking café or restaurant for coffee or breakfast.
- Get busy.

Before Bed
- If you have a partner, give each other a massage.
- Listen to a relaxation tape or CD.
- End your day with a little gentle yoga.
- Do a few good stretching exercises.
- Have the snack you planned *in advance*.
- Floss and brush your teeth with fancy toothpaste.

11 | Roadblock #6—Depression

All smokers endure an emotional roller-coaster ride of little mood swings throughout the day. Each cigarette is a trip that starts with an initial "kick" after lighting up—the best part of the smoke—but it's followed by a downhill slide of almost instant nicotine withdrawal. The slide is interrupted for a few seconds with each puff, but then it keeps going down until the next cigarette. Smoking may give some relief, but it's very temporary.

When people are depressed, the thought of giving up something that makes them feel better—even if the relief is as fleeting as a puff on a cigarette—can make them feel worse. This is one of the reasons why smokers who are "down," whether a little or a lot, have had difficulty quitting.

A few years ago Roy tried to quit smoking cold turkey and a depression he had struggled with when he was younger returned. His method for dealing with both the depression and nicotine cravings was to eat sweets. Eating sugar is one of the reasons many people gain weight when they quit smoking using conventional methods. Sugar is like nicotine—it briefly elevates the mood, which then plummets along with the body's glucose level.

Roy sometimes quit smoking for as long as two weeks, but his candy diet began to make him sick. He was also unhappy by what he thought was his co-workers' lack of interest in his progress. He didn't expect a lot, but he always felt let down by others—a feeling shared by many depressed people.

Before Your Quit Day

Depression often cycles depending on the day of the week or time of day. Many people feel worse in the morning and better as the day goes on; other people feel better in the morning and worse in the evening. Days off can be a problem for people who don't have enjoyable activities planned or if they're alone.

By identifying the times when you're most likely to be depressed, you can tailor your schedule to keep you busy and away from cigarettes. Just consider those times your "trouble spots," and use them as an opportunity to try out new activities.

On Your Quit Day

1. Give yourself plenty of small rewards.

   Make a list of things to help yourself along—your payoffs for not smoking on Quit Days. Here are some suggestions:

   - Keep a bottle of expensive water nearby. Don't drink this kind of bottled water on smoking days.
   - Make a quick phone call to a nonsmoking friend. Put together a list of several nonsmokers or quitters you can call, so you'll reach at least one of them. But the day will come when you can't reach anyone. When that happens, just keep going. You're doing fine without them.
   - Look at a book with a lot of photographs. Travel books,

HELPER

Don't Fill In Trouble Spots with Work

When you know a trouble spot is coming along, say, Friday night, be sure to have a few pleasant activities lined up. Don't dedicate Friday night to balancing your checkbook unless you like looking at the numbers in your bank account; don't clean your house unless you enjoy it. Sometimes it helps to get a chore or two out of the way because you feel better when an unpleasant task is finished, but be sure to end your work with a nonsmoking reward. You deserve a better one than a cigarette.

especially, can be helpful because they take your mind away from where you are and give you a few minutes of pleasant daydreaming. If, like Roy, you have always wanted to visit South America, you can dream about going there when you look at the pictures. You can put the money you're saving by not smoking into a fund for travel or for whatever else you want.

- Save magazines you subscribe to and read them only on Quit Days. Most people read at least one magazine, but if you don't, save the best parts of the Sunday paper for your Quit Day.
- Suck on hard candy, again, only on Quit Days. Hard candy is fat-free, and if you prefer, you can get the sugar-free kind.
- Chew gum—as much as you want and whenever you want—only on Quit Days. Gum can be a lifesaver. Bubble gum is good, too. You can crack gum, pop it, and blow bubbles—until people tell you to stop.
- Put special sugar or flavoring in your coffee or tea only on Quit Days. Making your coffee or tea special can pick up a Quit Day.
- Listen to your favorite music. That doesn't mean you shouldn't listen to music on other days, but favorite CDs should be saved for your Quit Days.
- Go out to dinner if you can. If you have to, go alone. Make sure the entire restaurant is nonsmoking. Make dinner on your Quit Night something special, whether you go out to eat, pick up something from your favorite sandwich shop, or fix your favorite meal. Make it special whether you're eating alone or with others.

Each of these rewards is small, but they add up. Having small rewards instead of large ones is important because you won't take them on smoking days. For example, it's unnecessary to drink gourmet bottled water that costs a lot of money. Even if you drink nothing except bottled water all the time, having water that's a bit fancier than usual is a very small reward, and you won't feel deprived when you drink the cheaper water on smoking days. The little things add up, just like your Quit Days.

Use as many little rewards as you can think of. They can get you through a Quit Day as long as you don't use them on your smoking days.

2. Steer away from temptation by keeping smoking supplies out of sight (the empty washing machine or clothes dryer are good places), and try to avoid smokers.

3. After the first Quit Day, quitters usually light up as usual. But sometimes, there's a little conflict. The cigarette isn't as good as they thought it would be, and they thought about going a little longer before lighting up again. After a few hours they are smoking as much as usual, but they're not smoking more than usual.

4. Think ahead to your next Quit Day and make plans to do something special. If your Quit Day is during a workweek, perhaps you could take in an early movie after work. You probably do most of your leisure-time activities on weekends, but consider switching some of your activities around so you can enjoy your smoke-free days as much as possible. This leaves you with less to do on weekends, but as you slowly get used to doing without cigarettes, you can explore new activities to keep busy—and not depressed—on weekends.

5. Find pleasant activities and keep busy doing them! It can help to make a list of little things you like to keep from being depressed, especially when you have a strong urge to sit and do nothing except smoke. There are books—humorous or inspirational—that can cheer you up. Keep a Bill Bryson travel book handy, or a *Far Side* cartoon book, or perhaps a book that inspires you.

Buy some TV sitcoms or films and save them for down times. There are audiotapes and CDs of stories and poetry narrated by actors with wonderful voices that will carry you away from your troubles for a while. The trick is to have them

---

IMPORTANT!

If you've been touched by depression, you know how you felt when you tried to quit smoking and failed. Perhaps that failure is also a way for you to "confirm" that you aren't "able" to quit, which only makes you feel worse.

If you have had bouts of serious depression, talk to a counselor or therapist before starting any quit-smoking plan. It's in your best interest to make certain you don't become more depressed if you try to give up cigarettes—even if the method is as gentle as the plan I've outlined.

---

handy and to *use* them when you need them so you can get out of that chair!

SUMMARY: ROADBLOCK #6—DEPRESSION

Before Your Quit Day
- Try to identify the times when you're most likely to be depressed. Tailor your schedule to keep you busy during those times and away from cigarettes.
- Make a list of little things you can do to feel better when you have a strong urge to sit and do nothing except smoke.

On Your Quit Day
- Have plenty of small rewards lined up for your Quit Days; for example: gourmet bottled water; a quick phone call to a nonsmoking friend; picture books on travel, art, or photography; magazines; newspapers.
- Suck on hard candy; chew gum.
- Put special sugar or flavoring in your coffee or tea.
- Listen to your favorite music.
- Go out to dinner to a nonsmoking restaurant, if possible. Whether you eat at home or in a restaurant, make dinner special.
- Keep smoking supplies out of sight, and avoid smokers.

> **IMPORTANT!**
> Overall, smoking makes depression worse, but if you are currently experiencing serious depression, you should wait to become a quitter.

- Think ahead to your next Quit Day and make plans to do something special.
- Keep busy.
- Read books—humorous or inspirational—that can cheer you up.
- Buy or rent some TV sitcoms or films and save them for down times.
- Search for audiotapes and CDs of stories and poetry.

12 | Roadblock #7— Unexpected Setbacks (Pies in the Face)

Sometimes everything in life is going along just peachy, when all of a sudden you get a pie in the face. Most of these surprise setbacks are just unpleasant, although some are hurtful. But the effects of a pie in the face are generally temporary, and after you tidy things up, you can usually get on with your life.

Disappointment is often unexpected, even when we've prepared ourselves for losing the girl or guy, the case, the contest, the lease, the raise, the promotion, the contract. Even when we knew it was a long shot, we're still let down because we hoped that all the stars just might be lined up in our favor, our luck would hold, we deserved it, and we wanted it so much.

Unexpected setbacks can transform a committed quitter into a relapsed quitter. It happens, and here's where this plan will get you back on the straight and narrow.

Setting Yourself Up for Relapse

After a sudden, unexpected setback, when your resolve to quit smoking is shaky and your self-esteem is flatter than a pancake, you sometimes end up with the last person you should be with. If, when you are emotionally vulnerable, you turn to a smoker for comfort, you have set yourself up for relapse.

Julie had been a quitter for several weeks when she and her boyfriend had a disagreement and, before she knew it, they had broken up. For consolation, Julie called her friend Dottie, a chain-smoker, and the two of them went to a coffee shop where Dottie could smoke. Julie was confident that she had control over smoking by then, but the part of her that was hurting really didn't care. When she asked Dottie for a cigarette, it was impulsive, because her life was suddenly in a slump and she needed a quick fix to ease her aching heart.

When Julie left the coffee shop after she and Dottie had smoked up a storm, she had to make a decision: Did she want to be a quitter no matter what was going on in her life? Did she want to be an occasional smoker? Or did she want to be a smoker for a few days or weeks, or until things changed in her life and she was ready to quit again? Fortunately for Julie, she and her boyfriend made up and there was a happy ending to their story and to Julie's efforts to quit smoking. But what happens when things go differently?

Using the Plan after Relapse

This plan leaves room for unexpected downers, and you can get through yours without having a full-blown relapse. For a few days you might spend a lot of your spare time with friends and relatives who smoke, but after you find the beginning of a small path to help you past this roadblock, you will be ready for a Quit Day.

1. Try just one Quit Day and see how you feel. If it makes you feel worse, you will either resume smoking for a while or decide that it's a good time to make some important life changes. You may not like it any more than Julie did when her aunt told her that "adversity is an opportunity to try new things," but when you feel better, you might find out that it isn't such bad advice.

2. Plan to smoke the day after your Quit Day. This is important! All that you have to deal with is one Quit Day. Don't move on to step two until you're ready. Don't bypass step two and skip to step three just because you were a successful quitter for several weeks or even months. Once you get off track, you can't quit cold turkey—you need to return to steps one and two. This means you will have smoking days alternating with

Quit Days until you're comfortable adding more Quit Days or quitting altogether.

3. Light up on smoking days, but if you don't want to, you shouldn't smoke your "usual amount." Try not to return to your old habits by making smoking a part of your emotional self-care. You deserve better.

4. If you can, substitute a pleasant activity for a cigarette. Think about something else you could do to take your mind off your troubles. See a movie (not a sad or upsetting one), talk to non-smoking friends, shop, and go where people don't smoke. Do a physical activity: walking, riding a bike, even driving to a new area and then exploring it on foot can make you feel better.

Waiting for the Unknown

Unfortunately, it happens: the checkup scheduled in two weeks, the court date next month, or perhaps an upcoming visit from friends with out-of-control children. This means that you're going to be a wreck for days or weeks to come. When that happens, you can't sit still and fret over something that's going to tear you to pieces; you have to haul out the big artillery. This is the time to get support.

There are several ways you can go, depending on your income and where you live. If possible, call a therapist, get in soon, and get some advice. Otherwise, it depends on the problem and how urgently you need to talk to someone. Here are some suggestions, but they are not your only resources. It's always best to find out what's available in your area *before* you need the service:

- Look up "Social Service Organizations" in the Yellow Pages. There's something there for everyone and every problem.
- Call your local university or college counseling service for recommendations. Ask about fees. The counseling service won't have too much information about outside costs, but they may be able to steer you to someone else.
- Hotlines: I've called hotlines about three times in my life, each

time for a different reason, and I've had varying results. If you don't get the help you want or need, try another hotline. Don't assume that the person at the other end of the line is an expert. If your gut feeling says you're talking to the wrong person or the wrong organization, get off the phone right away and call someone else.

- Pastoral counseling: In the old days, men and women went to seminaries to learn how to lead a congregation and preach. Counseling wasn't usually part of their training, and most religious leaders were not very good at counseling people. That's all different now. The people who lead your church, synagogue, mosque, or temple have been trained in pastoral counseling. Give it a try if you belong to a congregation, and if you don't, try someplace near you if you feel comfortable about it.

- Organizations such as NOW (National Organization for Women), AARP (American Association of Retired Persons), or a local organization for teens, for men with particular needs, for gays, for people with disabilities, or for just about anybody, including all kinds of ethnic groups, can provide assistance. Your phone directory has a Guide to Human Services section (sometimes blue-bordered pages) with the names and phone numbers of local organizations. There may also be a list of Self-Help Support Groups. Use them! They're there for us.

Bad days are a part of life. It's how we handle them that makes the difference between being perpetually miserable or miserable only sometimes.

You have survived every bad day in your life, and you can get through the next one without smoking.

SUMMARY: ROADBLOCK #7—UNEXPECTED SETBACKS (PIES IN THE FACE)
Setting Yourself Up for Relapse
After a sudden, unexpected setback, try not to set yourself up for relapse by turning to a smoker for comfort.

Using the Plan after Relapse
- Try just one Quit Day and see how you feel.
- Plan to smoke the day after your Quit Day.
- Light up on smoking days, but try not to return to your old habits by making smoking a part of your emotional self-care.
- Substitute a pleasant activity for a cigarette. See a happy or funny movie, talk to nonsmoking friends, shop, and go where people don't smoke.
- Do something physical: walk, ride a bike, or drive to a new area and explore it on foot.

Taking Care of Yourself
Find out what's available in your area *before* you need the service.

- Look up "Social Service Organizations" in the Yellow Pages of your phone directory.
- Contact national or local organizations you think might be helpful. Check your phone directory's "Guide to Human Services." In your area, this may be the same as Social Service Organizations.
- If you don't have someone to call for support, contact your local university or college counseling service for recommendations in your area.
- Hotlines—check them out before you may need them for yourself or for someone else.
- Seek pastoral counseling.
- Don't just sit there; take positive steps to feel better!

13 | Roadblock #8—Fast Food, Junk Food, and Overeating

People who quit smoking often turn to food as a substitute for a cigarette. That would be okay if the food they used to help them get over a cigarette craving were low in calories, fat, and sugar. Unfortunately, that usually isn't the case, and this is why many people who quit smoking using conventional methods gain weight.

If you are like Kate before she went on the plan, you may use your favorite fast food outlet—in Kate's case, Joe's Donuts, which was conveniently located two blocks away from her shop—to control cravings for cigarettes. Getting past these places without stopping can be difficult. You may promise yourself that you'll have only one donut or just a small burger and no fries, yet every time you stop at the counter, words come out of your mouth that you can't seem to control. After a few days, you force yourself to get on the scale to look at the somewhat alarming jump in numbers. It's usually enough to drive you back to cigarettes.

When quitters are faced with the double temptation of fattening food and cigarettes, they have three choices:

1. They can buy a pack of cigarettes and light up. They'll get a nicotine rush, which will help them stay away from the donuts.
2. They can forget about the cigarettes and buy the food so they get a carbohydrate rush. That won't last very long, and they'll soon regret their choice. They may feel bad enough that they will smoke after they eat the food.

   If they use cigarettes to keep away from food, they will feel bad, but they *won't feel as bad* as they would feel if they bought the food, and this is why people use cigarettes to help manage their weight.

What can quitters do?

On Your Quit Day

3. *SUBSTITUTE!* Take a direct detour from what your heart desires before you reach it!

Whenever you have a sudden desire for any combination of fat and sugar or cigarettes, immediately have something else. This is important because, while a little of most foods is okay for both your emotions and your body, that isn't what you're going to do on a Quit Day. A little bit leads to a lot. A lot leads to guilt. Guilt leads to giving up. Giving up leads to a cigarette. So take a detour and make a quick getaway.

That's a tall order, because when you're going by those special places we all know about: the bakeries, the fast-food stands, the pizza parlors *("Extra cheese, please"),* the shop that sells thirty-five different flavors of chips, or those glitzy aisles at the grocery store filled with things *that are meant to kill you,* there may be nothing in the world more enticing, more mouth-watering, than about two thousand calories.

Here's how you substitute:

- Zero in on the store across the street and spend a little money on something else: a magazine, a little treat for you or your partner or your mother-in-law.

  When you're trying to stay off cigarettes and fattening food, substitutes can keep you going until something comes along that either takes your mind off smoking or prevents you from smoking altogether. If you can find a way to put off a cigarette until you get into a nonsmoking coffee shop or department store, you won't be able to smoke until you leave. It's better to spend a few bucks on a glass of juice or a magazine than to spend three dollars on a bag of donuts, or more than that for a pack of cigarettes. In the meantime, the store will change your path and maybe distract you from your cravings. A change of pace can help get you through your Quit Day.

If you keep a mental list of your main temptations and one or two substitutes for them, that can help you in many moments when you are likely to succumb to the junk food or the cigarettes. For example, if you frequently hop in the car and drive to the mall and happen to end up in the food court where most of the food is very sweet or high in fat, make a plan ahead of time. Is there a place near the mall or even in the mall that has good-tasting, healthy snacks?

Take a trip to the mall and check things out before you have a Quit Day. If you can't resist the donut shop, make a plan to almost immediately head for the substitution. Planning ahead for trouble spots and finding substitutes before you need them helps you to stay away from fattening food and cigarettes.

- Eat what you enjoy but aren't addicted to. Walk over to Rosie's Diner and ask Bernie to make one of his famous sandwiches. You've already had breakfast, and if you eat the entire sandwich as a snack, you're going to take in a lot of extra calories, but assuming that you aren't addicted to sandwiches, you can eat something fairly healthy *("Hold the mayo please, and no chips")* and you can escape from the sugar-fat/cigarette trap—at least for now.

Kate avoided the donuts by ordering her favorite egg-salad sandwich, which she took to her shop and ate before she opened in the morning. Passing Joe's stand was a lot easier for Kate when she had something healthier than a donut for breakfast. Plenty of good food you are not addicted to can keep you away from the junk.

A sandwich could be your breakfast; that way, you won't be eating too many more calories than usual. When you eat one of those big muffins they sell in bakeries, you can take in close to a thousand calories. A healthy, low-fat sandwich containing protein and some vegetables isn't the worst breakfast in the world, and it can be one of the best. You can also take along some fruit, a bagel, a slice of good bread, bottled water, whatever you think will help get you past your food temptations and the cigarettes on the corner.

- Eat with discrimination. Stop at a nonsmoking café for a cup of mochaccino with a shot of chocolate. Something like that by itself isn't loaded with calories (unless you begin to take serious interest in the carrot cake they have in the case, so don't).

  Good food is substantial; it fills you up, and it is satisfying. Junk food just makes you want more. Like alcohol is to an alcoholic, junk food is addictive, it produces guilt, and it makes people throw in the towel, go whole hog, say "What the hell," and light up. The fat-sugar combo doesn't satisfy—it makes you want more and more until you're stuffed.

- This is not a day for dieting. You can't do both at the same time. Please remember that you're human. Don't go hungry on your Quit Day. You're better off eating well: three square meals and a snack.

- Take care of *you!* You are doing something very good for yourself and the people who care for you. You need to put yourself first for just a little while. Take care of everyone else on your smoking days. Your Quit Day is special.

- Have a snack on Quit night

  "Oh, good. Donuts from Joe's?"

  "Big pizza, double cheese? Maybe a hoagie?"

  No, something simple. Plan ahead for your snack and make it nice. Low fat and no sugar. Don't go after the leftover lasagna. Don't even have leftover lasagna in the house on your Quit Day if it's made with a lot of high-fat cheese and greasy meat. After you clean it up, you'll run out for some cigarettes and smoke. Or you'll just fall into bed and wake up the next morning feeling lousy.

  The problem with food cooked in fat is that it is addictive too. We eat a little and then we want more . . . and more. Compounding the damage, one ounce of fat has more than twice the calories of one ounce of carbohydrate or protein. Fat is delicious and fattening. What's worse is that even though you're getting more calories in high-fat food, your hunger may not be satisfied any more than if you were eating low-fat food. You don't get full sooner because of extra fat (good research shows this to be true). That's why fat makes you fat, and it's one of the reasons that life isn't fair.

Food is almost everywhere, and nowadays a lot of the food that surrounds us is fattening. Fattening food is addictive. Cigarettes are addictive. When you want to quit smoking without gaining weight, you'll be more successful at both if you make sure to do good things for yourself.

Always substitute!

If you're faced with the irresistible choice of either smoking or eating something whose only purpose on this planet is to make you fat, try to find an enjoyable substitute. The substitute will not be as good! But it will help you get through your Quit Days. As your Quit Days increase in number while your smoking days decrease, you'll have plenty of time to come up with more substitutes for cigarettes and fattening food.

Summary: Roadblock #8—Fast Food, Junk Food, and Overeating

Before Your Quit Day
Make a mental list of your main food temptations and one or two substitutes you can turn to almost immediately for each temptation.

On Your Quit Day
When you must choose between fattening food and a cigarette, *SUBSTITUTE!* Take an immediate detour from fast food and junk food by eating nutritious, low-fat, low-sugar food.

- Don't ever go hungry on a Quit Day and don't try to diet.
- Begin your very first Quit Day with a nutritious breakfast.
- Eat healthy, substantial food on your Quit Day: three square meals and a snack.
- Eat with discrimination: a cup of mochaccino with a shot of chocolate is better than a pastry. A cappuccino is even better.
- Eat what you enjoy but aren't addicted to.
- Stay away from fast food.
- Have a nice evening meal.
- Have a snack at night. Plan ahead for your snack and make it low fat and low sugar.
- Don't drink sugared soda pop or canned iced tea. They're full of chemicals (and a lot of empty calories).
- If you are away from home, buy a magazine or a little nonfood, nonsmoking reward if you want to smoke. Buy a healthy snack.
- Take care of *you!* Your Quit Day is special.

14 | Roadblock #9— Beverages: Coffee, Tea, Alcohol, Soft Drinks

"How about a glass of milk and a cigarette?" No thanks—unless the milk is topping off a cup of coffee.

"Fruit juice and a smoke?" Sure. As long as the juice is spiked with a jigger of vodka or rum.

Except for teenagers who smoke and drink soft drinks or canned, sweetened iced teas, the drinks of choice with a cigarette are usually coffee and alcohol.

Coffee

If you're a coffee drinker, you'll probably want to continue to enjoy it on your Quit Days. You can look forward to your coffee without a cigarette by planning ahead—just a little. One way to do this is to save special coffee for your Quit Day. It doesn't take much effort, but you'll get enormous pleasure out of drinking a good cup of coffee. Make sure to drink your special coffee only on Quit Days.

Before Your Quit Day

Buy good coffee. If you drink the stuff that comes from a can (and last saw the light of day heaven only knows how long ago), take some of the money you're saving by not smoking and go to the best coffee store in your area (probably not a supermarket or a chain).

Buy a pound of beans in a flavor you like, or try different flavors by buying a half-pound each of two or three flavors. Gourmet coffee isn't cheap, costing at least seven or eight dollars a pound, but it's less expensive than cigarettes.

On Your Quit Day
On the morning of your Quit Day spoon some coffee into the filter of your coffeemaker, turn it on, and if your coffeemaker is automatic, jump into the shower. When you get out, the aroma of good coffee will fill the air. If you use a stovetop coffee pot, you should stay in the kitchen until it's ready. You can busy yourself frothing milk, getting out the nutmeg, or listening to the news. If your coffeemaker has a timer, you can also set it up the night before so it will be ready when you wake up in the morning.

HELPER

Having a cup of coffee in one hand without a cigarette in the other takes a little getting used to. As you go through your Quit Day, keep in mind that tomorrow is a smoking day, even when you're having a cup of coffee without a cigarette. Hold something in your other hand: the newspaper, a magazine, a small photograph of a loved one, or a religious memento—whatever helps.

Tea
If you drink tea, you should enjoy your beverage on Quit Days. There are very good teas in wonderful flavors, both with and without caffeine. Regardless of the color of the leaf, green or black, tea is good for you. Tea contains polyphenols, chemicals that fight cancer and heart disease. Tea also has a lot less caffeine than coffee.

The best tea I've ever drunk—and I'm not much of a tea drinker—was at the café at the big mosque in Paris, where I sat outside at a table and drank tea that was fruity, sweetened a little with honey, and blended with all kinds of wonderful spices. It was delicious. A cigarette with good tea would ruin the flavor.

You can spend a lot of money on a tea ritual, or you can do it fairly cheaply. But you can't enjoy rewarding yourself like this if you smoke, because your taste buds won't know the difference between sludge and the good stuff.

On Your Quit Day
You might want to experiment with some of the many varieties and flavors of tea. Any good shop that specializes in coffee probably has a decent selection of fresh teas.

- Green tea has more polyphenols, which help to scavenge those unhealthy free radicals in your body. Drinking green tea on your Quit Day is a good way to remind yourself that you're doing something wonderful for your health. Some people drink a lot of green tea for its benefits, but even a cup or two can help your body.
- In cold weather it's nice to brew a cup of tea in a teapot and place a tea cozy over it while it steeps. After the tea is ready, you can put a little milk in the bottom of the teacup, then pour the tea over the milk.

On smoking days, drink tea made from a generic tea bag steeped in your cup. Save the good tea for Quit Days.

Soft Drinks, Sodas, Pop (It's all the same; it just depends on where you live)
A lot of people are hooked on soft drinks, and they have their drink with a cigarette—even in the morning.

Most teenagers who smoke usually have a soft drink along with their cigarette. Many of them make soda and a cigarette their breakfast. A lot of teenage girls drink diet pop and smoke to control their weight.

Yet this method of weight control is largely ineffective and may actually promote obesity in teens. When young people learn that it's comforting and gives confidence to have something in their mouths all the time, they spend more time eating when they aren't smoking and drinking sodas. Getting into the habit at a young age of keeping the mouth busy leads to obesity.

On Your Quit Day

1. Instead of soft drinks and cigarettes, take a bottle of water with you—whether you're in high school or as old as the Queen Mum who lived to be 101. If it makes you feel good, get ridiculously overpriced "boutique" water. Yes, you can think that you're throwing away money, and in some sense you are because there is usually perfectly good and safe water from the tap. However, if walking around with a bottle of Perrier or Poland Spring helps to keep you from smoking, then the trade-off is worth it.

   Having a bottle of water handy can help you to stay off both cigarettes and soda because the water is something to put in your mouth, and dealing with the bottle gives you an activity to replace smoking. It's also a reminder of good health.

2. You might want to take a small bottle of orange juice with you if the weather isn't too warm. Orange juice has nutrients you need: vitamin C and potassium. (Remember to keep the juice from getting warm or the vitamins will be destroyed.)

   Also, be sure to get *real* juice. There are a lot of "juice drinks" that contain as little as 10 percent fruit juice. The rest is corn syrup and chemicals the body doesn't need. Many juices, even the ones advertised as "healthy," contain corn syrup. Read the labels before you buy. Some tomato or vegetable juices are great but others have too much sodium.

Alcohol

Alcohol and cigarettes go together like shoes and socks, wine and cheese, or Ben and Jerry.

Many people are like Phil, who gets home from work and unwinds with a couple of beers, the evening news, and a cigarette. Almost every time he tried to quit smoking, he ended up overeat-

---

CAUTION!

Many people who attend Alcoholics Anonymous (AA) or Narcotics Anonymous (NA) meetings smoke, and ashtrays are usually provided. If you attend meetings for drug or alcohol addiction, don't stop attending because people are smoking. It's important for you to attend the meetings; however, this plan can help you to develop a strategy where you have Quit Hours rather than Quit Days.

---

ing junk food and drinking too much beer. Food and alcohol seemed to be his only weapons in his war on cigarettes.

His father had suffered from alcoholism and Phil didn't want to go down the same road. He had made a conscious effort ever since he was young to avoid drinking too much, and he wasn't going to take any risks. He wanted to quit smoking, his doctor wanted him to quit smoking, but Phil wasn't going to go from two cans of beer a day to a six-pack. This plan helped him avoid doing that.

On Your Quit Day

1. Plan Quit Day rewards that don't involve alcohol—which should never be used as a reward. Keep a supply of gum and hard candy to use only on Quit Days. Gum and hard candy can keep you going a little longer because you've got something in your mouth. If the candy is fat-free, as most hard candy and gum is, it's usually low in calories, although the trade-off is that you have to brush your teeth a lot or let your dental hygiene suffer for a while. Try sugar-free candy, especially if you have diabetes.

2. Plan to eat well on your Quit Day, but do it right. Some quitters overeat a little even with only one Quit Day a week. If overeating is a problem, make a list of all the foods you really like that are low in fat and fairly low in calories. Examples include chicken-breast sandwiches with light mayo, tomato, and lettuce; egg salad tofu sandwiches; tostados without the cheese

and sour cream; and gazpacho blended and stored in the refrigerator the night before your Quit Day. When you feel like having a drink to replace a cigarette, have a glass of juice. You can whip up some great juice drinks in either a juicer or your blender.

Use food to your advantage. Avoid fattening food and know what you like that can fill you up without putting on weight. Once you learn to enjoy good food on Quit Days, you can get through them without having a cigarette or turning to alcohol.

3. On Quit Days stay away from places where people typically drink: bars, lounges, cocktail parties, and groups where you know people are smoking. If you go to "test" yourself, you're going there to smoke. Anytime you do something to test your "willpower," you're on the road to giving in. Be aware of what you have done in the past. If you always smoked when you went to Cedric and Cynthia's parties, then you'll smoke the next time you go.

4. Don't schedule your first few Quit Days on the big game day! The combination of TV sports, alcohol, and smoking are so ingrained in some people, it's hard to pry them apart. About the last thing that comes to their minds when they are absorbed in a few hours of baseball, football, golf, or basketball is a cup of tea and a slice of Aunt Fannie's fruitcake. Put off scheduling your Quit Days on big game days until you feel comfortable watching TV without cigarettes.

5. Make Italian sodas at home with some soda water. They're very

---

CAUTION!

You don't want to change from a smoker who's trying to quit into a drinker. As Julia Child always said, things should be done in moderation, and you don't want to rely on alcohol to get off cigarettes. The probability of relapse is twice as great when quitters are drinking, so don't use alcohol to quit smoking.

good, you can try all kinds of flavors, and you can make them inexpensively. If you buy one in an upscale café, it will cost at least three dollars per glass.

6. Watch your salt intake. If you've been smoking for a few years, you should get chips with little or no salt. A diet high in sodium tends to raise a smoker's blood pressure. Bars serve salty snacks like pretzels to make you thirsty—so you will buy more drinks.

Enjoying Beverages without a Cigarette

The reminders for a cigarette aren't going away after you become a quitter; the daily rituals may still be in your life. This is a big challenge for quitters, and another advantage of this plan is that you will get used to enjoying your beverages without a cigarette, and—you'll have to trust me on this one—the day will come when you wouldn't want it any other way.

SUMMARY: ROADBLOCK #9—BEVERAGES: COFFEE, TEA, ALCOHOL, SOFT DRINKS

Coffee

Before Your Quit Day

• Buy good coffee in a flavor you like, or try different flavors by buying a half-pound each of two or three flavors.

• Save the good coffee for Quit Days.

On Your Quit Day

• Make your coffee as quickly as you can, or have it ready to turn on as soon as you get up. Don't sit around waiting for the coffee to be ready. Keep busy.

• When you drink your coffee, hold something in your other hand: the newspaper, a magazine, a small photograph of a loved one, or a religious symbol—whatever helps—until you become used to drinking coffee without a cigarette.

Tea

On Your Quit Day

- Use fresh tea you have bought from a specialty store.
- Use green tea as a reminder that you're doing good things for yourself on your Quit Day.
- In cold weather brew a cup of good, loose tea in a teapot.
- On smoking days, drink tea made from a generic tea bag. Save the good tea for Quit Days.

Soft Drinks, Sodas, Pop

Don't drink sweetened drinks to control obesity. It doesn't work.

On Your Quit Day

- Carry a bottle of water with you. If it makes you feel good, get expensive "boutique" water or water with a drop or two of fruit flavor.
- Carry some orange juice or any 100 percent juice in a thermos, or buy cold juice. Don't get sweetened "juice drinks."

Alcohol

On Your Quit Day

- Plan Quit Days that don't involve alcohol because drinking often leads to smoking.
- Keep several nonalcoholic rewards that you don't have at other times handy, including gum and hard candy.
- As an alcohol alternative, drink plenty of juice or mineral water. Make juice drinks in a juicer or blender only on Quit Days.
- On Quit Days stay away from places where people typically drink: bars, lounges, cocktail parties, and groups where people are smoking. (Never go to places where people are smoking to "test" yourself. Be aware of what you have done in the past.)
- Don't have your first few Quit Days on the big game day until you feel comfortable watching TV without cigarettes.
- Cut down on salty snacks because they cause unnecessary thirst and are bad for high blood pressure.

CAUTION!

If you attend meetings for drug or alcohol addiction, don't stop attending because people are smoking. Use this plan to develop a strategy where you have Quit Hours rather than Quit Days.

- Try Italian sodas.
- Don't rely on alcohol to get off cigarettes. The probability of relapse is twice as great for a quitter who is drinking.

You'll get used to enjoying your beverages without a cigarette, and before you know it, you won't want them any other way.

15 | Roadblock #10—Loneliness

Loneliness strikes everyone from time to time, but for some people, being lonely becomes an almost constant part of life. People who live alone are often victims of loneliness, but married people who spend most of their days by themselves in the suburbs sometimes feel stranded—no matter how lovely the house or how nice the neighborhood. Then there's the tremendous guilt *("Why am I so unhappy? I have everything anybody could ever want")* because the person who is supposed to have everything is lonely.

When Rachel's children were young, she spent all her time caring for them and her husband, who worked long hours. Now the children have left home, and Rachel's sister—her best friend—moved to Florida when her husband retired. Rachel ended up with an empty nest, a busy husband, and few friends. Although she had tried to quit smoking several times, her cigarette was often her only companion.

Rachel had heard about the plan from Rosie (who knows everything that's going on), but she didn't think that there was even one day out of the week when she could keep from smoking. She didn't want to bother trying something that she thought would fail.

This is a frequent complaint of lonely people—they begin to internalize their loneliness instead of doing something about it. If it drags on for too long, loneliness can turn into depression. Whether you live alone or are in a relationship where you feel lonely, you can take steps to make things better. Because you want to stop smoking you are showing a readiness to make some healthy changes in your life.

Before You Go on the Plan

1. If you're in a deep rut, do something to help yourself. Many people talk about how much they want to change their lives, but when it comes to doing anything to change the patterns of their lives, they'd rather not budge. Talking about things is no substitute for doing them.

   If you want to change something, try, even if you fail. Failure is okay. It's doing nothing that makes life stagnant, where nothing changes and nothing gets done. But while you're sitting around complaining about things, something *is* getting done. You are getting older, my friend. The clock isn't stopping, April turns into May, summer changes into fall, and that calendar is marking time. The more you fail, the more comfortable you'll be with the feeling—that concept is a key point in this plan. So take action. You will meet success along the way.

2. The quickest way to tune up your car is to take it to a mechanic. You can waste a lot of time—years—trying the same old stuff. You don't think twice about taking your car to a trained mechanic, but we can put off counseling because we think we can take care of things ourselves. Usually we can, but sometimes we need a sympathetic ear. Consider therapy as another tool to help make life a little better.

   If you decide to see someone, be sure that he or she is licensed and credentialed. I'm an advocate of counseling, but sometimes finding the right counselor is like shooting in the dark. But it's worth it: the right person can work with you to guide you out of the muddle you're in so you can get on with a better life. If you're lonely or depressed, a counselor can help you to feel better. That's why we have them.

On Your Quit Day

1. Get dressed, get out, get involved.

   This applies to anyone who is depressed, lonely, anxious, worried, stressed out, bored—in essence, feeling any negative emotions can shut a person down and lead to a condition of "inertia," an inability to do just about anything, especially anything that might lift the spirits. Inertia makes lonely people vulnerable to smoking, in spite of their deepest, truest, most heartfelt intentions to quit.

Before Rachel became a quitter, she was alone for most the day and watched TV, cooked, and read diet books. She had begun to binge eat, but she was always careful to make sure that no one knew. Often during the day Rachel sat on the sofa, looked out the window, and smoked.

Any quitter who sits around the house all day with little to do is probably going to smoke. It's important to get out and either go where smoking isn't allowed or to have a change of pace. On Quit Days, you need to get going, get involved, and get out!

Rachel decided to work for Rosie on her Quit Day because she couldn't smoke while she was at the diner. The mile-long walk from her house when the weather was nice made her feel as though she was doing something good for herself. And after a stop at the library on one of her walks home, she became a part-time volunteer stacking books—and she made some new friends. Rachel used the plan to quit smoking, but by using her own initiative she was able to ease her loneliness and become a quitter.

Sometimes it takes a little time to find your way, but with persistence you'll get there. Do what Rachel did and try one new activity at a time. If you don't like it, stop doing it; if you like it, you may be able to take on another activity after you become comfortable with your new routine.

2. Call old friends. Call someone you haven't had contact with for years. It can be a wonderful experience to pick up old threads and weave them into a renewed relationship. Sometimes it doesn't last; sometimes the two of you are in different places now. But just sometimes it does last, and for that reason, it's always worth a try. There are high school and college reunions, so why not have a reunion with people you've known and liked?

3. Volunteer for an organization such as your local library or

favorite charity. Most of them can use an extra hand, and they give you an opportunity to make new friends. There are also literacy groups that need people to tutor both children and adults. If you speak a language in addition to English, your help is especially needed.

4. If you don't have a pet, consider getting one. Animals don't like the smell of cigarette smoke, so if you need another reason to quit, your pet is a good reason. Pets get respiratory disease much more easily than humans, so don't smoke around your pet. Some of the world's best pets can be found at the local animal shelter or humane society. It's a great way to save a life and make a new friend.

5. Take a class at the local college or university. Most colleges offer a mind-boggling variety of courses both days and evenings. Learning more about something that has interested you can be fun, and it can also lead to a new hobby or career.

One quitter took a course in motorcycle maintenance and is now a certified mechanic. She is too busy running her own repair shop to be lonely—or to smoke.

Men Get Lonely Too

There is a misconception that women suffer from loneliness much more than men. Because women are often viewed as being more emotional, we may not realize that men can be lonely. But they can be, and loneliness hurts men just as much as it does women. If you go to any college counseling center, you'll find that as many male students seek help for loneliness and depression as females. The difference is that men don't talk about it as much, and that can be harmful.

Using an Alternative Plan to Quit

A few years ago, Drew left his hometown in the Midwest for Hollywood to act. He was poor, lonely for his family, his old friends—everything.

Quitting one day a week wasn't working for him because he was lonely every day. But he didn't give up; instead, he tried the alternative plan with a twist (see page 40) and lit his cigarette at twenty-two minutes past each hour—the date of his birth. He smoked whether he wanted to or not, and wherever he happened to be—without upsetting anyone or breaking any laws.

This alternative plan may be perfect for you. For one thing, even on lonely days, the alternative plan keeps you busy because you're timing your cigarettes *every* waking hour of every day. You may find that scheduling cigarettes is the easiest way for you to quit. If you ever slip in the future, you can quit when you're ready without feeling like a failure, without having to start all over again—by using your watch alarm to tell you when to smoke.

You may have to suddenly excuse yourself at odd times. Occasionally, Drew had to rush out of a building to smoke because he had lost track of time, but he didn't miss his cigarette. After a couple of weeks he quit entirely. For him, the icing on the cake was that he ran into an old friend who needed some technical help with a film, Drew gave him good advice, and he began an unexpected and successful career in the film industry.

SUMMARY: ROADBLOCK #10—LONELINESS

Because you want to stop smoking, you're showing a readiness to make some healthy changes in your life. You have taken a good step to reduce loneliness.

Before You Go on the Plan

- If you're in a deep rut, get out of it. Create some new patterns in your life. Don't keep going to the same old places and doing the same things you have been doing. You'll abandon some of the new activities; others may be unsuccessful. Keep trying. Failure is okay.
- If you think that counseling may help, give it a try. Counseling is simply another tool to add to your arsenal of helpers. Be sure the professional you see is licensed and credentialed.

On Your Quit Day

- Get up, get dressed, get out, get involved. Go where smoking isn't allowed.
- Try one new activity at a time. If you don't like it, stop doing it and find another.
- Call old friends.
- Volunteer for an organization: your library, a favorite cause, a literacy group. Tutor English.
- If you don't have one, consider getting a pet. Save a life and make a friend by adopting from the local animal shelter or humane society.
- Sign up for a college course. Talk to the nonsmokers.

16 | Roadblock #11—Missing the Pleasure of Smoking

Imagine a legal drug that relaxes you and gives you a sense of well-being, while at the same time boosting your energy and your metabolism. Thinking of cigarettes in this way makes smoking look awfully good, and all your reasons to quit may be hard to remember at times.

After quitters smoke their "last cigarette," memories of the pleasure of smoking don't magically disappear. Reminders to smoke are all over the place, and deciding to quit doesn't mean the entire world is going to help you out—or even care.

Phil tried to imagine what it would be like to never again feel the rush of smoke from his cigarette entering into all the pockets of his lungs, then coming back up and shooing out of his nostrils like two bullets. He loved to see the smoke drift away from him in marvelous curlicues and arabesques and float about the room like clouds. Phil could not imagine how he could spend the rest of his life without cigarettes. (Of course, he never pictured that after the smoke left his lungs, the residue would stay down in the delicate alveoli, or sacs, like a sticky tar.)

When you first quit smoking, you miss your cigarettes. They are friendly companions whose infidelity is hidden for years. A lot of people have spent more time with their cigarettes than they have with anyone in their family, and when they give them up, they give up a steady companion.

But cigarettes never go away. You can go out and get some anytime, almost anywhere. They're usually not too far away. What will keep you from smoking is the plan, a gentle, easy way to help you finally stop smoking for good—just as Phil did.

On Your Quit Day

1. Remember the bad times instead of the good. You'll think about cigarettes less and less the longer you go without smoking, but that "fatal" moment may come along when a cigarette can slide right into home plate. That's more likely to happen when you remember only the good times you had when you were smoking, instead of the nausea from too many cigarettes, the smell on your children, the bad breath, the burning in your throat, and the ashes and little burn holes in your clothes.

   When alcoholics who are on the wagon are asked to describe their drinking days, the ones who recall only the good times are more likely to relapse. People who remember the hangovers, the sickness, the lost work, and the humiliation are more likely to remain sober. It's the same for smokers on the wagon: if you keep in mind the unpleasant aspects of smoking, you'll be less likely to long for a cigarette.

2. Do the math! If you can't stop thinking about the pleasures of smoking on your Quit Day, distract yourself for a while by calculating the number of minutes left before you can smoke. Counting down while you're doing a task is more rewarding than counting up because you're heading toward zero—and the moment you can smoke. When you're having a Quit Day, zero is usually midnight (unless you're a shift worker and you don't go to bed until morning). But no matter how you carve it up, everybody has a twenty-four-hour day.

3. Read the "Reasons for Quitting" listed in chapter 21. You can photocopy this page so you can personalize it and keep it with you.

   Read the list out loud from time to time and keep reminding yourself why you want to quit.

   The next time you long for a cigarette, take a good hard look at a dirty, overflowing ashtray.

4. Also see chapter 20, "Reminders and a Few Tips." If you have children or grandchildren, or other people who love you, look at them (or photographs of them) and ask yourself if they de-

serve to lose you before your time. People care for you, and they want you around. Keep pictures of your loved ones handy. They can go a long way toward helping you reach your goal of quitting. And keep in mind that when you smoke around them, you're harming them as much as yourself because they are breathing very harmful secondhand smoke.

5. Don't forget the little rewards! Look at it this way: What you're doing is really quite wonderful. You are giving up cigarettes— something you've wanted to do for years. If going for an hour, a morning, a day, a week without smoking isn't worth giving yourself little gifts, then what is?

   Just keep in mind that if you keep associating small rewards (not big ones) with times when you're not smoking, then smoking will gradually lose its value, and being a quitter will mean more to you.

6. Save the good times in your life, as much as you can, for your Quit Days. You deserve plenty of good things to make them pleasant. If you get through an event that usually involves smoking without having a cigarette, reward yourself. Getting a lot of rewards when goals are met encourages meeting more goals.

   Quit Days are for your new good times. Smoking days are going to be a thing of the past.

SUMMARY: ROADBLOCK #11— MISSING THE PLEASURE OF SMOKING

On Your Quit Day

- Remember the bad times instead of the good: the nausea, the smell, the bad breath, the burning in your throat, and the ashes and little burn holes in your clothes.
- Keep in mind that cigarettes are unfaithful friends.
- The next time you long for a cigarette, take a good hard look at a dirty, overflowing ashtray.
- Do the math! Distract yourself by calculating the number of

minutes (and seconds and nanoseconds) left before your Quit Day is over.

- Keep pictures of your loved ones handy. They can go a long way toward helping you reach your goal of quitting.
- Don't forget the little rewards! Associate small rewards with not smoking. You deserve plenty of good things to make your Quit Day pleasant.
- Save the good times in your life, as much as you can, for your Quit Days.

Getting a lot of good things when goals are met encourages meeting more goals.

17 | Roadblock #12— Driving (On the Road)

Kate has always been on the go, and she always took her car. If she had to go somewhere only two blocks away, she'd drive there, and then spend fifteen minutes looking for a parking spot.

Kate has worked hard building her own business selling antiques and designer crafts. Because she's always on the lookout for unique merchandise, she spends a lot of time driving to garage and estate sales and artists' studios. For years she always had a cigarette locked between her fingers while she was on the road. Her car and cigarettes have gone together like a close-knit couple, and it was hard to separate them. Not smoking in her car was Kate's biggest challenge when she went on the plan.

She selected a Quit Day when she would be at home with her family, and she didn't have too much trouble until after dinner. Nevertheless, she made it to the next morning.

On the morning of her second Quit Day she had to drive out into the country to pick up a dozen handmade quilts to sell on consignment; after an hour on the road, she stopped and bought a pack of cigarettes. Because she still had little confidence in her ability to be a quitter, and she had little experience staying off cigarettes, once she smoked her quit plan flew out the window. She decided to make the following day her Quit Day for that week.

The Evening before Your Quit Day
This is the time to schedule a car wash so your vehicle smells fresh and clean on your Quit Day. Don't smoke until you get home so it stays fresh for the next morning.

IMPORTANT!

If you relapse on a Quit Day, don't make the following day your Quit Day unless it is scheduled. Most likely, you'll do what Kate did, who didn't smoke until nine o'clock in the morning, then she smoked for the rest of the day. Don't keep moving your Quit Day around. Stability and consistency are needed for long-term success. If you have two or three disappointing Quit Days, consider an alternative plan (see chapter 5).

What is a disappointing Quit Day? You'll know by the way you feel. Although you want to be a permanent quitter in the long run, perfection is not the most important goal in the short run if striving for it is stressful. The purpose of this plan is not to make you disappointed in yourself; the purpose is to help you reach small goals a step at a time.

On Your Quit Day

1. Practice makes perfect . . . even if it takes time. If you smoke one, two, three or more cigarettes on your drive, it is good practice to discard your pack as soon as you can. You can even park the car, smoke, throw the pack in a trash bin, and then resume your trip. If you need another cigarette, you can buy another pack and smoke another cigarette or two. If that seems like a waste of money, it's a lot cheaper than the price of a pack of cigarettes every day. You can also think about the best place for a cigarette: in the trash or in your lungs?

2. In an emergency, have Quit Hours. If you get stuck in your car on a Quit Day and cigarettes just happen to be in your car, you can have Quit Hours. If you know you'll be on the road, you can plan to smoke at certain times. Scheduling a cigarette, say, every twenty minutes while you're on the road helps to cut down on your smoking.

You need to know that you can set quit goals and meet them. The more quit goals you meet, the more confidence you'll gain in your ability to control your smoking.

3. Smoke during the trip, not before or after. If you keep having trouble when you're driving on Quit Days, buy a pack of cigarettes before the trip, smoke as much as you want during the trip—to your destination and back home—then throw away the remainder of the pack before your trip ends. That way, you always keep the house and your place of work off limits for smoking.

   If you live in an area where the inside of your car doesn't freeze in the winter or burn up in the summer when you aren't in it, put something in the ashtray, such as a plant, to remind yourself that you don't smoke now. Or you could, in a brave moment, remove the ashtray and throw it away, first making certain that anything in it is cold.

4. Take your helpers where you find them. Kate was afraid she would never be able to stop smoking while she was driving. She tried, but she couldn't stop taking a pack of cigarettes along with her when she was on the road. Then her daughters started nagging her. "None of our friends' moms have cars that smell like yours, Mom." They overdid it a bit, but that was enough to get Kate to stop smoking in her car.

   Do your children or significant others complain about the way your car smells? Maybe your friends are too polite, but if they always ask to open the window within the first minute of getting in your car—enough time for them to breathe the smell—you can be sure it's bothering them.

   Deodorizer just won't do it—it's only more chemicals covering up the stale odor. Your children and their friends have noses like police dogs.

Passengers Who Smoke

When other people ride in your car, don't let them smoke because of the proximity between you and their cigarette. Also, the lingering tobacco odor is a temptation you don't need.

Carpools

If you carpool and the driver smokes, you have to think like a nonsmoker who cannot tolerate being closed up in a smoky car. Nonsmokers find other, perhaps less convenient, ways to get to work. But they would not hesitate to leave the carpool if someone were permitted to smoke in the car. Start thinking like the nonsmoker that you are!

SUMMARY: ROADBLOCK #12—DRIVING (ON THE ROAD)

The Evening before Your Quit Day

Schedule a car wash so your vehicle smells fresh and clean on your Quit Day. Don't smoke until you get home so it stays fresh for the next morning.

On Your Quit Day

- If you smoke on your drive, discard your pack as soon as you can: make a stop and throw the pack in a trash bin, then resume your trip;

or

- If you smoke on your drive, schedule each cigarette for a certain time, say, every twenty minutes;

or

- If you keep having trouble when you're driving on Quit Days, buy a pack of cigarettes before the trip, smoke as much as you want during the trip—to your destination and back home— then throw away the rest of the pack before your trip ends.

- Throw away your car's ashtray or fill it with a plant.
- Don't allow people to smoke in your car.
- Carpool with nonsmokers or find another way to get to your destination—even if it's less convenient.

18 | Roadblock #13—The "Empty Hand" Problem

The "Empty Hand" is a serious issue. If you've been smoking a pack a day, you have been bringing your cigarette to your mouth about two hundred times a day! That hand, arm, and mouth is going to have to find something else to do, or else do nothing.

When Iris quit smoking before she used the plan, she sat on the sofa with one hand wrapped around a bottle of mineral water while the other hand tapped on the table where she usually kept her cigarettes. Tapping on the table wasn't going to get her very far, and after a few hours, she got into her car and drove to the store for a pack.

Iris's solution on her first few Quit Days was to keep busy with her painting students, teaching them how to mix paint, hold a brush, and stretch canvas. When she didn't have anything to do with her hands, she held on to her paintbrushes or the board she uses as a palette—whatever was available in her studio or the rest of the house.

After you quit, you'll have plenty of moments when you won't know what to do with yourself, your hands, your mouth (except eat another potato chip). How can you watch TV and sit in a chair with your hands at your sides as still as two dead fish?

The solution is to keep your hands busy and to spend time in places where you can't smoke until quitting becomes second nature. Rachel couldn't smoke at her new job at Rosie's Diner, and she couldn't light up at her volunteer library job either. Knowing that her first few Quit Days would last only hours instead of "forever" made quitting easier when she got home in the evening.

When Phil used other methods to quit smoking, he didn't know what to do with his hands either, especially when he was watching TV. Without his cigarettes, he usually had a bag of chips in one hand and a beverage in the other.

After Phil became a quitter, he played with worry beads and then a ukulele. This drove his family crazy because he played the ukulele badly and almost constantly. Phil was determined to keep cans of beer out of his hands on his Quit Days, so he switched to soft drinks. He still eats too many potato chips when he's watching the big game, but he doesn't smoke (and the chips are salt-free).

You'll have to deal with that extra hand when you become a quitter, but it won't bother you as much as it would if you were quitting "forever." On this plan you can make the lifestyle changes in such a gentle, nonabrasive way while you turn from smoker into quitter, you'll be able to deal with the little irritants.

On Your Quit Day

1. Make music. If you don't have one, buy a guitar (a cheap used one will do) and take a couple of lessons or teach yourself (Paul McCartney had to teach himself to play because he's left-handed). Play the piano or another instrument if you can; even a harmonica will keep your hands occupied and take your mind off cigarettes—for a little while. And with this plan, a little while is all you need.

   Play hand drums or the bandoneón—an accordion-like instrument often heard in tango music. If you learn how to play it, you can prepare for the tango lessons you'll want to take after you become a quitter. Maybe actor Robert Duvall will invite you to the tango studio he has converted from a barn on his farm.

   Go to a music store and buy a kalimba. It's small and portable, easily carried in a large handbag or briefcase, and you can tap out sounds that are pleasing to the ear. Originally from Africa, the kalimba sounds like a small xylophone and is sometimes played in Caribbean music.

Don't make music on smoking days. Save your music for Quit Days. Roy likes music, especially tango and bossa nova; he's always happy when he listens to Stan Getz and Charlie Byrd. And on his Quit Days, which are every day now, Roy plays Getz, Byrd, Virginia Rodrigues or whoever else is new on the South American music scene.

2. Sometimes one good thing leads to another. Roy's interest in Latin music got him to sign up for a course in Spanish, which he hadn't spoken since high school. He's planning a month-long trip to Argentina, Brazil, and Chile next year, and he wants to be able to get around without too much trouble. He also wants to dance—if he gets up the nerve.

3. Write poems or stories. Do creative writing only on Quit Days. Have a Quit Day diary. If you publish it, you probably won't make as much money as the latest biographer of the stars, but you'll enjoy writing it, anyway.

4. Knit, sew, or crochet. You need both hands for this kind of work, and you don't want your creation spoiled because it smells like tobacco smoke. It may help to buy good wool yarn at an upscale yarn shop. That way, you're much less likely to knit or crochet when you are smoking.

5. Type. You run the company? Type anyway. Typing keeps both hands busier than just about anything else you can do. Typing really helps because your hands are in constant motion and you can expend some of that nervous energy on the keyboard. Don't do fancy drawing and painting with your computer; you want to keep those fingers flying. Forget about typos; you can correct them later if you want. If you're doing personal typing, write letters to friends and relatives. Now is also a good

---

CAUTION!
Make sure that you keep cigarettes away from your computer and work area, and keep your fingers on the keys!

time to give the press, including the Internet, an earful (or eyeful) of what you think.

After you become a quitter, your smoking hand is probably going to weigh about thirty pounds and sprout three other hands with seventeen fingers for a while. Sometimes you won't know what to do with them. Typing something, anything, is a great substitute for a cigarette because it keeps all of your fingers busy.

After a few Quit Days you'll get used to not having a cigarette between your fingers, but this won't happen overnight. Your brain will slowly reprogram your fingers so that they won't miss them at all. Eventually, the idea of holding a cigarette will seem like a burden.

Summary: Roadblock #13—
The "Empty Hand" Problem
On Your Quit Day

- Keep something in your smoking hand: a pen, pencil, paintbrush, coffee cup, pictures of loved ones, magazines, books—this book.
- Keep both hands busy: typing, juggling, orchestra conducting.
- Keep food out of your hands unless it's good for you.
- Make music: play the piano, guitar, harmonica, hand drums, bandoneón, small kalimba—or whatever you want.
- Type. Type. Type. Make those fingers fly. No smoking around the computer.
- Knit, sew, crochet. Use good wool yarn you would hate to ruin with cigarette smoke.

19 | Roadblock #14—Lack of Confidence (Insecurity)

The tobacco industry has tried to convince us that we look more sophisticated, confident, self-assured—in other words, all those qualities we wish we had all the time—when we've got a cigarette between two fingers. This has been accomplished through the use of movies, TV, sports, magazines, and newspapers, all of which have willingly helped give tobacco a cachet of glamour. Many famous and beloved celebrities have smoked; some of them have advertised tobacco, and a few of them still do in foreign markets. (That way, unless you travel extensively, you don't have to know about it.) Beautiful, sexy screen sirens have often used cigarettes to add a touch of danger to their beauty; popular television shows geared directly to young people have pushed smoking. I can think of two popular sitcoms that blatantly used tobacco to milk a few laughs, including one in which a female star smoked a cigar.

Cigarettes have little bands of gold and brand names to remind us of royalty. In real life, there's a Duke of Kent in England, and there was a Duke of Marlborough. Winston Churchill was the British prime minister who led Great Britain through World War II, looking happy as a clam with his ever-present cigar. The British government is called Parliament, and officials sent from England to govern the colonies—parts of Africa, Asia, and India—were called "viceroys." The man who first mass-produced cigarettes was an American with a royal name: James B. Duke. We're reminded that smoking helps to keep women slender, and sometimes women are led to believe that they can get the guy if they have a cigarette between their fingers. Some brands remind men of their virility or how much fun it would be to be a cowboy.

As a result, holding a cigarette when you're unsure of yourself is a confidence booster. The cigarette makes it look like you're taking some time out from the gathering, and you *could* join the group if you wanted, but you have made the choice to withdraw for a while—and smoke. At least, that's what you're thinking.

Social insecurity happens to everyone. In awkward moments, smokers can look for their cigarettes, pull one out of the pack, light it up, and puff away. Smoking sometimes makes it look as though people *choose* to isolate themselves for a few minutes in order to take care of a preferred activity. Without a cigarette, unless they're one of those people who are good at "working the room," a cigarette is used to fill uncomfortable time.

What most people don't do in uncertain social situations is run over to the buffet and stuff themselves with food. Eating is associated with gluttony, while smoking usually doesn't have the same social stigma unless a smoker is thought of as inconsiderate. Eating a lot at a party makes us look pitiful. In contrast, going to the porch for a smoke appears to be a well thought-out choice.

From time to time throughout life, almost every person you have ever seen or known has suddenly been placed in an awkward social situation. Smokers use cigarettes to keep busy. They can stand around with a cigarette until they get their bearings or someone approaches them to talk. When nothing is working in a room, or if there is no smoking inside, smokers can always go outside where, because of the shared isolation of smokers, they can strike up a conversation with someone puffing on a cigarette.

Think back to the most embarrassing moments of your life. There were probably many throughout the years, but most of them have been forgotten. When you try to remember the most embarrassing moments that happened to someone else, you can probably recall few—if any.

There are many times and occasions when people feel self-conscious, but no one else is saying to themselves or each other,

"That poor thing has no one to talk to." The only discomfort is what you feel inside, so your feelings of discomfort are what you have to deal with, not what other people are thinking about you. Smoking *does* leave an impression—the impression that you smoke. You don't want that to be your signature. When you feel awkward at a party, keep the following in mind:

1. People don't talk about another person simply because the person isn't in a conversation at the moment.
2. People who are standing around puffing on a cigarette, holding a drink, and looking off into the distance *are* leaving an impression, but maybe it isn't the impression you want to make.
3. You can feel comfortable if you have a glass of mineral water in your hand, a pleasant expression on your face, and a willingness to circulate and find the most interesting person in the room—more comfortable than if you are smoking. Try it!
4. This won't last forever (that's what a lot of the guests are thinking, not just you).
5. You can still go outside when you feel uncomfortable and find someone to talk to because there are people out there who are not smoking. When you feel a little more comfortable, you can go inside and ask for a soda or a glass of water with ice and a twist of lemon.

When you're on this plan, your self-assurance and good feelings about yourself will grow because of the tremendous achievement and success you're having as a quitter. Many of life's problems aren't going to disappear, but overall, you're going to have a better, healthier, and longer life.

SUMMARY: ROADBLOCK #14— LACK OF CONFIDENCE (INSECURITY)

Your only discomfort is what you feel inside, so your feelings are what you have to deal with, not what other people are thinking about you. When you feel awkward at a party, keep the following in mind:

- People don't talk about another person simply because the person isn't in a conversation at the moment.
- Smoking may leave a negative impression on others.
- Hold a glass of mineral water in your hand, keep a pleasant expression on your face, and find the most interesting person in the room. That person probably is not smoking.
- Remember that many people in the room are hoping to escape as soon as possible.
- You can go outside and find a nonsmoker to talk to. When you feel a little more comfortable, you can go inside and ask for a soda or a glass of water with ice and a twist of lemon.

Social insecurity happens to everyone. Your self-assurance and good feelings about yourself will grow because of your success as a quitter.

Part 3 | TIPS TO KEEP GOING

20 | Reminders and a Few Tips

Here are a few reminders and tips to help you get through the rocky spots of your Quit Days. All of them are important, but because everyone is different, some of them will matter more to you than others.

Keep Your Environment Tobacco Free
Help yourself out by keeping cigarettes, ashtrays, lighters, and other items that remind you of smoking out of sight. If possible, ask people who are nearby to help by keeping their cigarettes and ashtrays out of sight as well. Be sure to reward their cooperation with thanks and an occasional cup of coffee. If you have the bad luck to be near an unpleasant person who smokes, you may not be able to do anything about it. But it gives you the opportunity to associate cigarettes with unpleasantness.

Find Supportive People
All you need from others is an occasional friendly "How are you doing?" or "How are the Quit Days going?" If you want to talk about your progress, it's a big help when others show interest without overdoing it. Be sure to tell them how much you appreciate their support! As you go through a few weeks on the plan, you will find that people will tell you about friends and relatives who have been trying to quit smoking, and they will want more information about the plan to pass along.

Know the Difference between Bribes and Rewards

Bribes are usually onetime "payoffs"; rewards are given frequently for positive change and to maintain the change over the long haul. For this to be accomplished, positive behavior has to be rewarded frequently.

If you want to save for a big purchase, set aside your Quit Day cigarette money, but also give yourself frequent small rewards for not smoking. You want to meet the long-term goal of being a permanent quitter, but you also want to reward daily successes.

Remember, You Are Terrific!

As you go through the day without smoking, tell yourself, "I deserve good things. My lungs deserve good things. I deserve a better life than one where I'm always stuck to a cigarette."

Keep Track of Any Smoking on Quit Days

You had a cigarette on a Quit Day? Mark it down and then praise yourself for smoking less. If you didn't smoke less, praise yourself for keeping track. Keep track to know if you should go to an alternative plan.

Have Many Small Rewards on Quit Days

When you're a new quitter, you want as many rewards on your Quit Days as you can think of. Make sure that they're small, easy to get, and within your budget. Be liberal with your rewards. Make sure that when you use food as a reward, you eat delicious, healthy food that is well prepared. Setting a nice table with a tablecloth and good dishes can make your meal more pleasant, and it doesn't add calories.

If you use chewing gum as a reward, you may prefer sugar-free gum; if you use hard candy to get past a cigarette craving, one piece can last for several minutes. By then, you can move on to another kind of reward for getting past the craving.

Eventually, you won't have to go out of your way to find rewards because you'll be in the habit of being good to yourself—which includes not smoking!

Exercise: More Than a Tip

I know what some of you are thinking, but take a quick look at the following:

Exercise should be taken seriously for three reasons. First, there's an important link between exercise and a longer life. In a study that lasted for decades, men who lived longest didn't smoke and they exercised. Men with the shortest lives smoked and got little exercise. Your body is like a car: the better you take care of it, the longer it lasts.

Second, people who maintain a regular exercise routine have an easier time staying off cigarettes, alcohol, drugs, and excess food. Exercise helps to put you on a positive track for your life. You have to admit that there is something contradictory about working out and smoking. Even a brisk walk can sometimes turn you away from a cigarette.

The third reason for you to exercise is that in life after cigarettes, there are lots of empty spaces that you used to fill with smoking. You're going to stuff the empty nooks and crannies of your days with something. Mild exercise can be the mortar that fills some of those little spaces and keeps you from turning to unhealthy alternatives like overeating.

Experiment with different kinds of exercise until you find something you like. The key to making it work is to slip it into your life—and to keep it there without making a big deal out of it. Exercise has to be comfortable, just like this quit plan.

Many couch potatoes find health clubs they like. Some people are more comfortable walking, running, or swimming. Others find activities such as rock climbing or hockey or soccer leagues to keep active. Each of us is different, and each of us enjoys different things. You don't have to follow the pack.

After several failed attempts at learning how to swim, Carolyn finally found a very patient young man at her local YMCA who helped her get over her fear of the deep end. Carolyn said that swimming changed her life—more energy, no lingering urge to smoke, and both she and her son formed new and lasting friendships with other YMCA members.

When you learn how to do something physical that you've never been able to do, and you love it, your life gets a huge boost. And your body says thank you. Eventually, you may find that the feeling that comes with exercise is what you really like, perhaps even more than the actual exercise. That's okay. Making exercise a priority in your life is what's really important. Otherwise, it's too easy to let it slide. And scheduling it can be helpful for many people.

Until you clean out your lungs and make life easier on your heart, you might try walking. That's good, mild exercise to get you started. (Of course, talk with your doctor before starting an exercise program.) Roy used to drive around the parking lot until he could get a spot that was close to a store. Now he easily walks fifty city blocks and nothing hurts except his feet.

To make walking interesting, Drew bought a pedometer and now keeps track of his mileage on a calendar. Every time he clocks thirty miles, he treats himself to a new hardcover book. He can afford it now, and the miles pile up quickly since he started to run. Sometimes he's tempted to get two or three books, but he buys just the one and puts the others on hold, which gives him greater incentive. Every time you walk a few miles, give yourself a little treat: a new magazine, the latest mystery, a video. The miles can add up fast. You certainly don't have to make thirty miles your goal before you get the treat, especially when you're starting out. If you can't make it very far, that's okay. Start by walking to the corner or around the block. Do just a little more than what you've done before.

But here's the really important thing:

Don't give up on your exercise plan
for more than a few minutes! (or maybe a day).

Tomorrow will be another day whether you like it or not.

Take a yoga class, if possible. Watch the older people do what you'll be able to do when you aren't smoking.

See what's going on in your neighborhood. Check out your local pool or health club. Make the most out of what you have. YMCA's have financial aid programs for people who can't afford the full membership fees. Don't hesitate to ask. If you don't ask, you'll never know.

Consider playing a team sport through a local league—lacrosse, baseball, hockey, roller hockey. Think about taking lessons in boxing or karate, or learn to ballroom dance. If inline skating is too scary, try roller skating or ice skating. If you can, go hiking or hill climbing. You can't do these activities very well if you smoke, but think about the cardiovascular benefits you get out of climbing a gentle hill! And consider joining a club—ski, bike, and dance clubs are all over the country.

21 | Your Reasons for Quitting

On the following page is a sample list of reasons to quit smoking. Spend some time thinking about your personal reasons to quit and add them to the list. You are encouraged to photocopy the list so you can take it with you. Carry the list wherever you go and use it to remember why you're quitting. "Helpers" are also listed, and you may want to add your own, such as an inspirational verse or a favorite quote. Read this list of helpers throughout your Quit Day.

You've just had a cigarette? Read the list. Remember, this is a sample list—you can change it to suit your own needs.

Why I'm Quitting
- I want to smell better.
- I don't want to be chained to a pack of cigarettes.
- I like my teeth and gums. Smoking is destroying them.
- I'd like to see my children (or my grandchildren) grow up.
- I'd like to enjoy my coffee break—standing on the sidewalk is NOT fun.
- I'd like to save all the money I'm spending on cigarettes.
- I'd like to go out and not worry about having enough cigarettes.
- I'm sick and tired of finding ashes all over my car, butts in my ashtray, and burn holes in my clothes.
- I don't want to have a heart attack.
- I don't want to get cancer.
- I don't want to spend the last months of my life fighting for breath.
- I deserve better.
- Other reasons:_____
  _____
  _____

If you've photocopied this page, turn over your copy and continue the list of personal reasons you have for quitting on the back. The information on this page can be as personal as a diary, or you could make a list of words that would help you keep going.

Helpers
- My best qualities:_____
  _____
  _____

- Tomorrow morning I'm going to have a cigarette.
- Colonel Sanders was turned down by 1,600 people before he got his business started. If he could keep trying, so can I.
- Success comes to failures who don't give up.
- I'm not quitting forever, so I can handle it.
- Each new day is a new opportunity to be a quitter.
- In a few minutes I'm going to have a treat.

Another tool to help yourself as you use the plan in this book is to always replace thinking about a cigarette with a positive thought about yourself.

"Well, I can't think of anything right now because I want a cigarette."

I know.

Carry your photocopied page with you wherever you go. Read your good qualities and the words of encouragement several times a day.

You just had a cigarette? Read the page! There's more good to you than can be contained on one page.

Yes, there is.

22 | It's About Time

- There are 1,440 minutes in a day. Count down from time to time, as Roy did, while you go through the day. Part of the time you'll spend sleeping, and if you sleep for 8 hours, you can carve off 480 minutes, which leaves you with less than a thousand minutes (960, to be exact).
- There are 24 hours in a day. If you multiply 24 by 7, you have a total of 168 hours in a week. Let's assume that you get 8 hours sleep a night. If you sleep less than that, or more, you can adjust the numbers. Going by the 8-hours-a-night assumption, subtract 56 hours from the total number of hours in a week for sleep, and you're left with 112 waking hours in a week.

  For every hour you're not smoking out of the 112, give yourself a check mark on a chart or a calendar. Some people put a penny, marble, or chip in a jar for every hour of abstinence (for counting purposes); you may prefer some other way. Because you probably finished your last cigarette between the hours, say 10:23, you might even want to get a watch with an alarm and time from hour to hour.

  At the end of every hour without a cigarette, have a small treat—even if it's just a few swigs of overpriced bottled water. Say something nice to yourself like, "I did a good job." Tell others that you just went for an hour without smoking. You'll probably get praise, but don't brag too much to the smokers or they'll give you verbal punishment and offer you cigarettes. If you ride above them, they'll admire your efforts and some of them will try your method for themselves.

- There are 52 weeks in a year. If you multiply 112 by 52, the total is 5,824 hours you're awake a year (more or less, of course). Make a chart for the year and make a check mark for every waking hour you go without smoking. When you see a cluster of check marks showing that you didn't smoke, write down the total and reward yourself. You might want to put aside a dollar, or whatever you can afford, for every hour or day you don't smoke. You could take a nice trip a couple of times a year with the money you've saved.

What if you neglect your chart for a while? Leave the blanks and keep going—but don't reward the blanks. Just draw a line through them.

- Using my plan, you are tracking time spent not smoking and time spent smoking. Sometimes you smoke; sometimes you don't. If you quit for six months and then pick up a cigarette, call each day you smoke a smoking day. Tomorrow might be a Quit Day. Incorporate quitting into your life so that if and when you have a cigarette after several Quit Days or Quit Weeks or Quit Months or even Quit Years, it's NOT A BIG DEAL.

What's the point? You have felt like a smoking failure for a long time now; yet most of the time you're not a smoker. You're a person who sometimes has a cigarette. Period. Your primary payoff is one of the most powerful of all: TIME.

Whether we're rich, poor, lucky, or unfortunate, good health is something we have to work at every day of our lives. No exceptions.

A Final Word

Anything that's going to work over the long haul has to be convenient and fit into your life the way it is *now*. If it's inconvenient and uncomfortable, it will probably fail. This plan is for life. Quitting smoking isn't a thrill, but this plan makes it as painless as possible.

You now have the tools to stop smoking. What you have learned has cost you no more than the price of this book. You didn't have to sign on at an expensive clinic; you didn't have to do a lot to change your life; you didn't have to take medications. The benefits you'll get from quitting are without measure. The pain caused by smoking is without measure as well.

I hope that this method for quitting is as easy for you as it has been for the majority of people who have used it. No matter how quickly or slowly you progress, you can honestly call yourself a quitter. And you'll never have to start all over again.

May your nonsmoking days be plentiful.

Index

About the Author

Sandra Rutter, Ph.D., is a trained psychologist who has conducted extensive research on addiction. Dr. Rutter has an M.A. in research psychology from San Francisco State University and a Ph.D. from the University of New Hampshire (1990). She has extensive research and teaching experience at several colleges and universities and has published papers about addictive disorders in several academic journals. She is a former smoker.